1991–1995 E

MW01688470

Suggested Solutions

Land Law

LLB

University of London
External Examinations

HLT Publications

HLT PUBLICATIONS
200 Greyhound Road, London W14 9RY

Examination Questions
© The University of London 1991, 1992, 1993, 1994, 1995
Solutions © The HLT Group Ltd 1996
Reprinted 1999

All HLT publications enjoy copyright protection and the copyright belongs to The HLT Group Ltd.

All rights reserved. No part of this publication may be reproduced or transmitted in any form or by any means, electronic, mechanical, photocopying, recording or otherwise, or stored in any retrieval system of any nature without either the written permission of the copyright holder, application for which should be made to The HLT Group Ltd, or a licence permitting restricted copying in the United Kingdom issued by the Copyright Licensing Agency.

Any person who infringes the above in relation to this publication may be liable to criminal prosecution and civil claims for damages.

ISBN 0 7510 0723 4

British Library Cataloguing-in-Publication.

A CIP Catalogue record for this book is available from the British Library.

Printed and bound in Great Britain.

CONTENTS

ACKNOWLEDGEMENT

The questions used are taken from past University of London LLB (External) Degree examination papers and our thanks are extended to the University of London for the kind permission which has been given to us to use and publish the questions.

Caveat:

The answers given are not approved or sanctioned by the University of London and are entirely our responsibility.

They are not intended as 'Model Answers', but rather as Suggested Solutions.

The answers have two fundamental purposes, namely:

1. To provide a detailed example of a suggested solution to examination questions, and
2. To assist students with their research into the subject and to further their understanding and appreciation of the subject.

Note:

Please note that the solutions in this book were written in the year of the examination for each paper. They were appropriate solutions at the time of preparation, but students must note that certain caselaw and statutes may subsequently have changed.

INTRODUCTION

Why choose HLT publications?

Holborn College has earned an international reputation for the outstanding quality of its teaching, Textbooks, Casebooks and Suggested Solutions to past examination papers.

Our expertise is reflected in the outstanding results achieved by our students in the examinations conducted by the University of London LLB Honours Degree Programme for External Students, the Council of Legal Education, and by students in over 70 universities who use our publications.

Suggested Solutions

The Suggested Solutions series provides examples of full answers to the problems posed by examiners. The solutions are much more than answers achievable by a candidate under examination conditions. The opportunity has been taken, where appropriate, to develop themes, suggest alternatives and set out additional material providing further comprehensive topical coverage.

To aid comprehension and revision, the solutions are fuller than would be possible under examination conditions. It is important to keep in mind that at this level there almost certainly is more than just one approach in answering any given question.

We feel that in writing full opinion answers we can assist you with your research and further your understanding and appreciation of the law.

Notes on examination technique

Although the SUBSTANCE and SLANT of the answer changes according to the subject-matter of the question, the examining body and syllabus concerned, the TECHNIQUE of answering examination questions does not change.

You will not pass an examination if you do not know the substance of a course. You may pass if you do not know how to go about answering a question although this is doubtful. To do well and to guarantee success, however, it is necessary to learn the technique of answering problems properly. The following is a guide to acquiring that technique.

Time

All examinations permit only a limited time for papers to be completed. All papers require you to answer a certain number of questions in that time, and the questions, with some exceptions carry equal marks.

It follows from this that you should never spend a disproportionate amount of time on any question. When you have used up the amount of time allowed for any one question STOP and go on to the next question after an abrupt conclusion, if necessary. If you feel that you are running out of time, then complete your answer in note form. A useful way of ensuring that you do not over-run is to write down on a piece of scrap paper the time at which you should be starting each part of the paper. This can be done in the few minutes before the examination begins and it will help you to calm any nerves you may have.

Reading the question

It will not be often that you will be able to answer every question on an examination paper. Inevitably, there will be some areas in which you feel better prepared than others. You will prefer to answer the questions which deal with those areas, but you will never know how good the questions are unless you read the whole examination paper.

You should spend at least 10 MINUTES at the beginning of the examination reading the questions. Preferably, you should read them more than once. As you go through each question, make a brief note on the examination paper of any relevant cases and/or statutes that occur to you even if you think you may not answer that question: you may well be grateful for this note towards the end of the examination when you are tired and your memory begins to fail.

Re-reading the answers

Ideally, you should allow time to re-read your answers. This is rarely a pleasant process, but will ensure that you do not make any silly mistakes such as leaving out a 'not' when the negative is vital.

The structure of the answer

Almost all examination problems raise more than one legal issue that you are required to deal with. Your answer should include the following:

Identify the issues raised by the question

This is of crucial importance and gives shape to the whole answer. It indicates to the examiner that you appreciate what he is asking you about.

This is at least as important as actually answering the questions of law raised by that issue.

The issues should be identified in the first paragraph of the answer.

Deal with those issues one by one as they arise in the course of the problem

This, of course, is the substance of the answer and where study and revision pays off.

If the answer to an issue turns on a provision of a statute, CITE that provision briefly, but do not quote it from any statute you may be permitted to bring into the examination hall.

Having cited the provision, show how it is relevant to the question.

If there is no statute, or the meaning of the statute has been interpreted by the courts, CITE the relevant cases

'Citing cases' does not mean writing down the name of every case that happens to deal with the general topic with which you are concerned and then detailing all the facts you can think of.

You should cite only the most relevant cases – there may perhaps only be one. No more facts should be stated than are absolutely essential to establish the relevance of the case. If there is a relevant case, but you cannot remember its name, it is sufficient to refer to it as 'one decided case'.

Whenever a statute or case is cited, the title of statute or the name of the case should be underlined

This makes the examiner's job much easier because he can see at a glance whether the relevant material has been dealt with, and it will make him more disposed in your favour.

Having dealt with the relevant issues, summarise your conclusions in such a way that you answer the question

A question will often say at the end simply 'Advise A', or B, or C, etc. The advice will usually turn on the individual answers to a number of issues. The point made here is that the final paragraph should pull those individual answers together and actually give the advice required. For example, it may begin something like: 'The effect of the answer to the issues raised by this question is that one's advice to A is that ...'

Related to the previous paragraph, make sure at the end that you have answered the question

For example, if the question says 'Advise A', make sure that is what your answer does. If you are required to advise more than one party, make sure that you have dealt with all the parties that you are required to and no more.

Some general points

You should always try to get the examiner on your side. One method has already been mentioned – the underlining of case names, etc. There are also other ways as well.

Always write as neatly as you can. This is more easily done with ink than with a ball-point.

Avoid the use of violently coloured ink eg turquoise; this makes a paper difficult to read.

Space out your answers sensibly: leave a line between paragraphs. You can always get more paper. At the same time, try not to use so much paper that your answer book looks too formidable to mark. This is a question of personal judgment.

NEVER put in irrelevant material simply to show that you are clever. Irrelevance is not a virtue and time spent on it is time lost for other, relevant, answers.

UNIVERSITY OF LONDON
LLB EXAMINATION 1991
PART I
for External Students

LAND LAW

Monday, 3 June: 10.00 am to 1.00 pm

Answer *FOUR* of the following *EIGHT* questions

1 'There is no justification today for retaining two methods of creating settlements of land.'

Discuss. If a single method is to be adopted, what form should it take?

2 In 1980 Peter granted a lease of a house to Thomas for a term of 30 years subject to covenants to pay rent, to keep the house in a good state of repair and not to use the house for business purposes. Performance of the tenant's covenants was guaranteed by a surety, Simon. In 1989 Thomas granted a sublease of the house to Richard for a term of ten years and in 1990 Thomas assigned his lease to Stephen. In 1991 Peter assigned his reversion to Arthur.

Arthur has received no rent this year, the house is in urgent need of repair and Richard is proposing to start a business in the house.

What remedies does Arthur have, and against whom?

3 As Ann and Liza were close friends and were doing the same post-graduate course, they decided to share a flat. After looking for a month they found a two-room flat belonging to Lionel which suited them. Lionel insisted on each of them entering into separate but identical 'licence' agreements. Each agreement provided that the licence was to run for nine months from 1 September 1990 and that the licensee agreed to pay £200 per month as licence fee as well as 50% of the outgoings on the flat. The agreement further stated that the licensor should retain a key to the flat and that he reserved the right to occupy the flat whenever he wished. The agreement denied that the licensee was to have exclusive possession of the flat or any part of the

flat. Ann and Liza each signed their agreements and entered into possession of the flat on 1 September 1990. Nine months later Lionel told them to leave and, when they refused, he began making abusive telephone calls to them in the middle of the night.

Advise Ann and Liza.

4 In 1980 Mr and Mrs Hall purchased a cottage as their matrimonial home. The price of the cottage was £60,000, of which Mr Hall provided £30,000, Mrs Hall provided £20,000, and Mrs Hall's mother, Norma, provided £10,000 as a wedding gift for the couple. The cottage (the title to which was not registered) was conveyed into Mr Hall's sole name. In 1987 Mr Hall mortgaged the cottage to the Quickfix Bank in order to raise some money to invest in his brother's construction business. Mrs Hall knew about the mortgage, but, when the bank's representative came to inspect the cottage prior to granting the mortgage, she was away on a week's holiday. Recently Mr Hall has started to default on his mortgage payments and the bank is threatening to bring possession proceedings with a view to selling the cottage.

Advise Mrs Hall as to her position. If the cottage was sold, how would the proceeds of sale be distributed?

5 In 1984 John and Karen met and became lovers. At the time they were both married and living with their spouses, but they both hoped to obtain divorces and then to marry each other. In 1985 Karen became pregnant by John and John purchased a flat for her to live in. Karen gave up her job, left her husband and moved into the flat. Shortly afterwards she gave birth to a daughter, Clare. The flat was conveyed into John's sole name and he paid both the deposit on the purchase price, all the bills and all the repayments. For three years John provided Karen with the financial support for herself and Clare. In 1988 Karen found a good job and thereafter supported herself and her daughter as well as spending some money on maintaining and decorating the flat. On one or two occasions Karen asked John why he did not put the flat in their joint names, and he replied that it was because of his tax position, but that she had no reason to worry because she could stay in the flat for as long as she wished and because he was leaving her the flat in his will.

In 1991 John was killed in a car crash. In his will he left his entire estate to his wife, Wilma. His executors now seek possession of the flat with a view to selling it.

Advise Karen.

6 Peter owned a house at No 12 Church Street and Quentin owned the neighbouring house at No 14 Church Street. The titles to both properties were registered under the Land Registration Acts. In 1975 Peter erected a tool-shed partly on his own garden and partly on a strip of the garden of No 14 without Quentin's consent. In 1985 Peter sold No 12 to James who continued to use the shed and in 1990 Quentin sold No 14 to Henry. Henry now wants James to remove the shed.

Advise James. How would your advice differ if the land was unregistered?

7 'Once a mortgage always a mortgage and nothing but a mortgage. The meaning of that is that the mortgage shall not make any stipulation which will prevent a mortgagor, who has paid principal, interest, and costs, from getting back his mortgaged property in the condition in which he parted with it.' (per Lord Davey)

Explain this statement and consider the extent to which it remains true today.

8 Pat was the owner of Blackacre and Whiteacre, two adjoining pieces of land. In 1978 Pat leased Blackacre to his friend Mick for ten years at a rent for the purpose of growing vegetables and Pat covenanted to keep the fence which separated the two properties in a good state of repair. In 1980 Mick asked Pat if he could store his tools in a shed on Whiteacre and Pat agreed. In 1982 Mick asked Pat if he and his friends could play football on Whiteacre on Sundays and Pat agreed. In 1988 Pat died, leaving his entire estate to Rob. Rob has now refused to allow Mick to store his tools or to play football on Whiteacre, and Rob has also refused to repair the boundary fence.

Advise Mick.

QUESTION 1

General Comment

Although this is not a difficult question for a reasonably well-prepared student, it is probably one which most students would have been better advised not to attempt. Essay questions are deceptively difficult to answer well in examination conditions and it is all too easy to spend a lot of time and words in saying very little of real significance. Certainly anyone who had not read the Law Commission paper on Trusts of Land should have chosen another question.

Skeleton Solution

What was the historical justification for two systems? – Do these reasons apply today? – Main characteristics of the SLA settlement – What are the main problems of the SLA? – Is there still a need to retain the SLA? – Is the trust for sale always appropriate? – What alterations should be made to the trust for sale? – Conclusion: suggest single system based on the trust for sale but with some modifications.

Suggested Solution

The reason for the present dual system of creating settlements of land is historical. The original idea behind a settlement under the SLA 1925 (and its predecessors) was to retain land in the family, in circumstances where the life tenant would be residing on the property and would require wide powers of management in order to deal with the settled land to the best advantage of all interested persons. The land was likely to be a large estate. By contrast, the idea behind the trust for sale was to create a mechanism for holding land as an investment pending a sale of the land. Considerable differences remain between the two systems but it is by no means clear whether the existence of these differences justifies the retention of both systems.

The legal estate under an SLA settlement is held by the tenant for life and he will make all the management decisions concerning the property, including the decision whether or not to sell. It is impossible by s106 SLA to interfere with his exercise of these powers in any way. Under a trust for sale the legal estate is held by the trustees and they will make all the management decisions, although they may delegate the powers of leasing and management to the beneficiary. The legislation still gives priority to the SLA so that if no proper advice is taken, it is possible to have an SLA settlement by mistake – this is because if successive interests in land are created, there will be a settlement under the SLA unless an 'immediate binding trust for sale' is created, so that a home-made will which leaves a house to the widow for life and then to the children will create an SLA settlement with its attendant expense and complexity. It seems that a grant of a right of residence for life will also create an SLA settlement: see *Bannister* v *Bannister* (1), *Binions* v *Evans* (2).

The Law Commission identified several problems with the working of the SLA in their report on Trusts of Land. The system is complicated and expensive to administer with the requirement for two documents, a vesting deed and a trust instrument, and the need to take out a special grant of probate when the tenant for life dies. Further problems arise with settlements created accidentally under the SLA as these are bound to be improperly created without the required two documents. Conveyancing difficulties arise if it is not clear whether the settlement is under the SLA or a trust for sale as it is unclear whether the tenant for life of trustees should execute the relevant documents. There may well be a conflict of interest between the personal wishes of the tenant for life and the interests of the other beneficiaries and the latter are in a very weak position with no real right to object to the exercise of his powers by the tenant for life.

The conclusion of the Law Commission was that strict settlement under the SLA be abolished. The recommendation was made on the basis that there was no longer sufficient justification in retaining two parallel systems. The historical reasons for two systems no longer applied and research undertaken by the Commission showed that hardly any new settlements were created under the SLA in any event. The mechanism was cumbersome and expensive and its only advantage was that in some cases it was more appropriate for the tenant for life than the trustees to manage the settled property. The Commission suggested granting an enhanced power of delegation to trustees instead. The old reason for a settlement under the SLA was to keep land in the family and this is easier to achieve with a trust for sale by requiring consents to be obtained before sale.

However the Commission did not simply recommend that the trust for sale become the single possible system for creating trusts of land. The trust for sale is used in settlements with successive interests and when concurrent interests exist. In the latter case the trust for sale is an artificial concept. The Law Commission suggested that the type of co-ownership envisaged in 1925 would have been the situation of land being left to children in a will, when a sale would have resulted. In modern cases of co-ownership the land is purchased for occupation primarily rather than as an investment. The doctrine of conversion which applies to trusts for sale is incomprehensible to non-lawyers.

The recommendation was that the strict settlement and trust for sale should both be replaced by a new single system which would apply to all trusts of land, including bare trusts and concurrent interests. The land would be held by trustees with a power to retain and a power to sell. The doctrine of conversion would not apply. The powers of the trustees would be based on those of the absolute owner. The advantages of the new single system would be that it would remove the complexities inherent in a dual system and many conveyancing difficulties would disappear. In most cases it is more appropriate for the trustees to exercise the powers of management, but there would be improved delegation powers if it was wished that the life tenant should manage the property. The new system would be more in accord with the expectations and understanding of the lay person as it applied to co-ownership.

In conclusion, it is difficult to find any real justification for retaining the two systems of settling land and the scarcity of new SLA settlements in practice seems to confirm this view. The historical reasons for the two systems no longer apply. Therefore in the interests of simplicity a single system is preferable. If a single system is to be adopted, the trust for sale is certainly a more appropriate choice than the strict settlement, which is really of little practical relevance today, but there are significant problems with the trust for sale itself. Therefore a new system based on the trust for sale with certain changes is suggested. The emphasis on the duty to sell and the doctrine of conversion would be abolished and the trustees given power both to retain the land and sell it. This system, as put forward by the Law Commission, would be closer to the layman's understanding of the position.

References

(1) [1948] 2 All ER 133
(2) [1972] Ch 359

QUESTION 2

General Comment

A fairly standard question on the enforceability of leasehold covenants which covered privity of estate and contract and remedies available to the landlord. The well-prepared student should have had no real difficulty in coping with any of the points raised.

Skeleton Solution

Has benefit or covenants passed to A? – LPA 1925 s141, privity of estate – No privity between A & R? – Has burden passed to S? – Enforcement procedures against S: for failure to pay rent and other covenants – Is there a forfeiture clause? If not, breach of condition? – s146 procedure – Can A proceed against T? – Does benefit of S's covenant run with freehold?

Suggested Solution

There is privity of estate and contract between the original landlord and tenant, both of whom remain liable to each other on the covenants in the lease throughout the term. Thomas, as original tenant, remains liable on the covenants in the lease even after he has assigned the lease to Stephen. Arthur is not the original landlord but the assignee of the reversion and in order to enforce the covenants he must show first that the benefit of the covenants has passed to him. By s141 LPA 1925 the benefit of all covenants 'having reference to the subject-matter' of the lease pass with the reversion to the assignee. Such a covenant is said to touch and concern the land or affect the landlord in his normal capacity as landlord or the tenant in his normal capacity as tenant. The covenants in this question are to pay the rent, to keep the property in good repair and not to use the property for business purposes. All these covenants are classic examples of covenants which touch and concern the land and thus the benefit of the three covenants has passed to Arthur.

Arthur may not bring proceedings for breach of covenant against Richard as although the benefit of the covenant has passed to Arthur there is no privity of estate or contract between him and Richard. Richard is only the sub-tenant. As the user covenant is a negative one, it might be directly enforceable against Richard under the law of restrictive covenants, but insufficient information is given to enable this possibility to be considered further. Whether Richard is in breach of his sub-lease, depends on its terms.

In order to enforce the covenants against Stephen, Arthur must show that the burden of the covenants has passed to Stephen and that there is privity of estate or contract between them. At common law the burden of covenants in the lease which touch and concern the land pass with an assignment of the lease (*Spencers Case* (1)). All three covenants touch and concern the land. There is no privity of contract between Stephen and Arthur as they are not the original parties to the lease but there will be privity of estate provided that the lease and the assignment were both legal and not merely equitable. Thus Arthur may enforce the covenants against Stephen.

Arthur may enforce payment of the rent directly by an action for the money or by seizing Stephen's goods through the procedure of distress. He may also be entitled to bring proceedings for forfeiture. The lease is only subject to forfeiture if the covenants are framed as conditions or there is a forfeiture clause in the lease. It is standard for a lease to contain an express forfeiture clause. If there is a forfeiture clause in the lease, Arthur must first make a formal demand for the rent, unless the lease exempts him from so doing. Stephen may obtain relief from forfeiture if he pays the rent due and any costs incurred by Arthur, provided that it is just and equitable to grant relief. The application for relief must be made within six months of the landlord obtaining judgment. If there is at least six months rent in arrears, Stephen has a statutory right to have the proceedings stayed if he pays the arrears of rent and costs before trial. Forfeiture of the lease will automatically determine the sublease to Richard, although Richard has a right to apply for relief independently.

Arthur may sue for damages for breach of the repairing covenant and for an injunction in respect of the user covenant (although this will be of little benefit as Stephen has not himself committed the breach), but he may be entitled to bring forfeiture proceedings if there is a forfeiture clause in the lease. He must first serve notice under s146 LPA 1925 and the notice must specify the breach, require it to be remedied if possible, and require the tenant to pay compensation, if the landlord requires compensation. Arthur must allow Stephen a reasonable time for compliance and three months would probably be sufficient. Certain breaches are considered incapable of remedy but both these breaches are capable of remedy. Stephen may apply for relief on such terms as the court thinks fit and relief is normally granted if the breaches have been remedied. By taking forfeiture proceedings Arthur may indirectly enforce the user covenant against Richard as if the lease to Stephen is forfeited, the sublease will determine. Richard has his own right to ask for discretionary relief.

The performance of the tenant's covenants was guaranteed by Simon as surety. In *P & A Swift Investments* v *Combined English Stores Group* (2), the House of Lords held that the benefit of a surety covenant could run with the reversion if the surety guaranteed performance of tenants' covenants which themselves touched and concerned the land. Provided that the surety given here was not expressed to be personal (whether given to Peter alone, or in respect of Thomas' personal obligations only) the benefit will pass to Arthur. The remedy against Simon will be in damages only.

References

(1) (1585) 3 Co Rep 16a
(2) [1988] 2 All ER 885

QUESTION 3

General Comment

This was a predictable question on the lease/licence distinction with particular reference to sharing arrangements. Students who had actually read the relevant cases would have had a definite advantage in answering the question.

Skeleton Solution

Is it a lease or licence? – Importance of distinction re security of tenure – Any remedy for harassment under Protection from Eviction Act 1977? – Is there exclusive possession? – Main cases on sharing agreements: joint tenancy or licence? – Is the term reserving to Lionel the right to occupy a sham? – Are separate obligations to pay fatal to a joint tenancy? – Conclusion: suggest on balance points more towards a lease but emphasise this area of law changing all the time.

Suggested Solution

The real issue in this case is whether Ann and Liza are tenants or licensees. If they are tenants they may be entitled to security of tenure under the Rent Acts, whereas if they are licensees, their rights depend on the terms of the licence and they will have no security of tenure as the Rent Acts will not apply. Whether they are licensees or tenants they may have a remedy against Lionel's abusive telephone calls under the Protection from Eviction Act 1977. This Act makes it an offence to harass a residential occupier with the intention of causing him to give up his occupation.

Therefore Ann and Liza may be able to prosecute Lionel under this Act, but this will not help them remain in occupation although it may give them some personal satisfaction.

A lessee must have exclusive possession and if there is no grant of exclusive possession there is no lease, although it is possible to have exclusive possession but still a licence. In *Street* v *Mountford* (1) Lord Templemann said 'Where the only circumstances are that residential accommodation is offered and accepted with exclusive possession for a term at a rent, the result is a tenancy.' The court will construe the agreement made by the parties and if, in substance, the agreement is a lease, it is a lease, no matter that the parties have called it a licence. In *Street* v *Mountford* the agreement was held to create a lease even though it clearly stated that it was only a licence. In this case the crucial question is whether Ann and Liza have been granted exclusive possession and the fact that the agreement calls itself a licence is not decisive.

There have been several recent cases on the difficult issues raised by multiple occupation and sharing agreements. Where there are several occupiers there may be a grant of exclusive possession to them all as joint tenants, or there may be no grant of exclusive possession so that all the occupiers are merely licensees. A third possibility, which does not seem to have been argued in the cases, would be that each occupier has a grant of exclusive possession of his own room with a shared right to use the common parts. In *AG Securities* v *Vaughan* (2) there was a six-roomed flat occupied by four persons. Each occupier signed an individual 'licence' agreement and the amount he paid depended on which room he occupied. There was a fairly high turnover of occupants and when one left, either the remaining occupiers found a replacement or the owners advertised for a replacement. A new occupier had to be acceptable to the owners. It was held by the House of Lords that this arrangement created a series of licences not a lease. It was not possible to say that there had been a grant of exclusive possession to the occupiers together. The occupiers had no right to exclude a new occupier introduced by the owners when one occupier left and this term to allow the introduction of new occupiers was clearly not a sham. The four unities essential for joint tenancy were not present. Different occupiers arrived at different times, paid different amounts and stayed for different periods. The argument that when one occupier left, his agreement was terminated and there was an implied surrender by the others followed by a new grant, was considered 'unreal' by the House of Lords.

This case is different to that of *AG Securities* in many respects. There is a term that Lionel may occupy the flat whenever he wishes, but that may well be a sham here. The flat has only two rooms and it is unlikely that it was ever intended by anyone that Lionel would actually move in. In *Antoniades* v *Villiers* (3) the owner granted a 'licence' to an unmarried couple to occupy a two-roomed flat and purported to reserve the right to go into occupation with the couple or introduce another occupier, but the House of Lords said that there had been a grant of exclusive occupation as this term was never intended to be acted upon and was a sham. It seems that in this case both Ann and Liza would have signed or neither. It does not seem to be material that they are two ladies rather than an unmarried couple. In *Hadjiloucas* v *Crean* (4) two ladies agreed to take a two-roomed flat with kitchen and bathroom. Each signed a separate agreement to pay and to use the flat with one other person and if one agreement was terminated the owner could require another person to move in. A retrial was ordered by the Court of Appeal but Lord Templemann in *AG Securities* clearly thought that this arrangement had created a lease with exclusive possession.

One problem does arise as each has a separate obligation to pay. Joint tenancy requires unity of obligation. In *Antoniades* v *Villiers* there were separate obligations to pay but Lord Templemann still held that there was a joint grant of exclusive possession. He said 'A tenancy remains a tenancy even though the landlord may choose to require each of two joint tenants to agree expressly to pay one-half of the rent.' However in the later case of *Mikeover* v *Brady* (5) the fact that there were separate obligations to pay was regarded as a fatal objection to any finding of joint tenancy. In that case there were two 'licence' agreements which imposed separate obligations to pay, although the agreements did not contain any express power to introduce new occupiers and the occupiers did not have the right to leave early on notice. Although the agreements appeared to grant joint exclusive occupation, the Court of Appeal held that there was no joint tenancy because of the separate obligations to pay.

Again in *Stribling* v *Wickham* (6) there were three separate agreements to use premises on a shared basis. It was held that the court must consider all the circumstances and construe the agreement in the light of the circumstances. Here each occupier was responsible for his own payment only and could terminate his own agreement on 28 days notice without affecting the rights of the others. Occupiers changed from time to time and the agreements were not leases but true licences as there was no grant of exclusive occupation. By contrast in *Nicolaou* v *Pitt* (7) there was held to be a grant of exclusive possession and hence a lease in a sharing agreement. In that case the court considered that there had been no real contemplation of introducing another occupier.

Thus some factors in this case seem to point towards a lease and some towards a licence. Ann and Liza appear to have exclusive possession despite Lionel's retention of a key and the term that allows Lionel to occupy the flat with them seems to be a sham as one cannot imagine that the parties ever intended it should be acted upon. However the existence of two separate obligations to pay points away from a joint tenancy and thus towards a licence. If the court is prepared to construe the two agreements together as in

Antoniades v *Villiers* it is likely that a lease exists. On balance this situation seems closer to *Antoniades* v *Villiers* than *AG Securities* v *Vaughan* or *Stribling* v *Wickham*. Both the latter cases were situations of a fluctuating number of occupiers when each occupier clearly was independent of each other. Here the two agreements appear to be dependent on each other, there is no provision for one of the occupiers to leave early, and the term allowing Lionel to occupy looks like a sham. Therefore it is suggested that Ann and Liza may well have a tenancy and thus protection under the Rent Acts and security of tenure. This area is one where the law is still changing and subsequent cases may point more firmly towards a lease or towards a licence. Lionel would have been better advised to use the new provisions of the Housing Act to grant a short-hold tenancy with guaranteed recovery of possession at the end of the term. Whether they have a lease or licence, Ann and Liza probably have some remedy against Lionel under the Protection from Eviction Act in respect of his abusive telephone calls.

References

(1) [1985] 2 WLR 877
(2) [1988] 3 WLR 1205
(3) [1988] 3 WLR 1205
(4) [1987] 3 All ER 1008
(5) [1989] 3 All ER 618
(6) [1989] 27 EG 81
(7) [1989] 21 EG 71

QUESTION 4

General Comment

It is to be hoped that not too many students talked about overriding interests here as the question clearly states that title is not registered. Although the problems raised by the issues in the question are well-known, there is often a tendency to overlook unregistered land and the doctrine of notice and concentrate on registered land and overriding interests.

Skeleton Solution

Does Mrs Hall have an equitable interest and if so, is it binding on the bank? – Legal title in Mr Hall but presumption of resulting trust applies – Does Norma have an interest or did she intend a gift? – What are the original equitable interests? – Unregistered land, so enforceability depends on notice – *Caunce* v *Caunce*, *Boland* – What are requirements for purchaser without notice: see *Tizard* – If no notice, bank not bound by Mrs Hall's interest – If bank has notice, does Mrs Hall's consent to mortgage mean that she cannot assert her interest against bank? – How should proceeds of sale be divided?

Suggested Solution

Mrs Hall needs to establish whether she has an equitable interest in the cottage and if so, whether her interest is binding on the bank as mortgagees. Mr Hall has the sole legal title as the cottage was conveyed into his name alone. However as Mrs Hall provided part of the purchase price there will be a presumption that the cottage is held on trust for the parties in proportion to their respective contributions. Mr Hall provided one half of the purchase price, Mrs Hall one third and the remaining one sixth came from Mrs Hall's mother. It seems unlikely that Mrs Hall's mother has an equitable interest in the cottage since she provided £10,000 as a wedding gift for the couple and therefore there will not be a trust in her favour. Is Mrs Hall entitled to a one third or some larger share?

It may well be that the intention of the parties was that they would be jointly entitled and that Mrs Hall has a half share in equity. She might argue that the gift from her mother was primarily to her although expressed as a gift to the couple, and thus that her contribution is one half of the purchase price. In any event her contribution is at least £25,000 out of £60,000 and it is suggested that the court is likely to find that the couple are entitled to half shares in equity. Is Mrs Hall's interest binding on the bank? She could have registered a Class F land charge to protect her right of occupation under the Matrimonial Homes Act but it seems that she did not do so, or the bank would not have granted the mortgage. Her equitable interest exists behind a trust and its enforceability depends on the old doctrine of notice. Mrs Hall needs to show that the bank had actual, constructive or imputed notice of her rights.

In *Caunce* v *Caunce* (1) the house was conveyed into the name of the husband alone although the wife was entitled to a half share in equity. Unknown to the wife the husband mortgaged the house to Lloyd's Bank. It was held that the bank took free of the wife's equitable interest as a purchaser for value of a legal estate without notice. This decision was criticised by the House of Lords in *Williams & Glyn's Bank* v *Boland* (2) concerning registered land, when it was held in similar circumstances that the wife had an overriding interest binding on the bank under s70(1)(g) LRA 1925. It is clearly not desirable to have the rights of the parties dependent on whether or not the land is registered. The later decision of *Kingsnorth Finance Trust* v *Tizard* (3) is also relevant. In this case the house was again conveyed into the sole name of the husband, although the wife claimed an equitable interest by virtue of her contribution. The marriage broke down and Mrs Tizard started to sleep at her sister's house on some nights. However she still slept at the matrimonial home on her husband's frequent absences and always went there early in the morning to get the children's breakfasts and ensure they were ready for school. She returned there in the afternoon and prepared the evening meal and went away if her husband came back. She kept most of her clothes there. Mr Tizard applied for the mortgage and arranged that his wife and children would be away when the valuer called to inspect one Sunday afternoon. Although on the application form he had described himself as single, he told the valuer that he was married but separated. The valuer's evidence was that he saw signs of occupation by Mr Tizard and the children but not by anyone else.

It was held that Mrs Tizard's interest was binding on the mortgagee as on the facts it was not a purchaser without notice. Mrs Tizard was still in occupation although she did not always sleep there, but in the case of unregistered land occupation in itself is not decisive. The reference to a separated wife, especially since Mr Tizard had previously said he was single, and the presence of the children should have alerted the valuer to make further enquiries. If the mortgagee carried out a proper inspection and did not find a person in occupation, or any evidence of occupation by that person, the mortgagee would have no notice of the rights of that person. An inspection at a time arranged by the mortgagor was not necessarily enough, but it depended on the circumstances of the case. Here the inspection had not been adequate.

In this case Mrs Hall was away on holiday when the inspection was made. It is not known whether the bank knew that Mr Hall was married, or whether there were any children. In *Kingsnorth* the court considered that the mortgagee should be alert for signs of occupation by other persons but that it was not necessary to open drawers and cupboards. It is suggested that if the bank knew that Mr Hall was married, or should have seen signs of occupation by Mrs Hall on the inspection, or had detected Mr Hall in making contradictory statements, the bank probably had notice of her rights. However if Mr Hall claimed to be single and there were no signs of occupation by anyone else, it may be that the bank can claim to be without notice of the rights of Mrs Hall.

A further problem is that Mrs Hall apparently knew of the mortgage, although she may not have known of its extent. There have been a number of cases where a wife has signed mortgage documents and later claimed that the mortgage was not binding on her. There is no presumption of undue influence between husband and wife. In *Cornish* v *Midland Bank* (4) a wife was held entitled to damages for negligent advice when the bank failed to advise her of the full meaning and effect of a mortgage, but the mortgage itself was not set aside as the bank had not taken an unfair advantage. In *Kingsnorth Trust* v *Bell* (5) the mortgagee could not enforce the mortgage against the wife as her signature was obtained by the husband's misrepresentations. The mortgagee had instructed the husband to obtain his wife's signature and so was liable for any misrepresentations he made. The mortgagee should have insisted the wife had independent legal advice.

This problem is rather different as Mrs Hall has not signed anything. If the bank had no notice of her occupation it will not be bound by her rights, but if it had notice, will Mrs Hall be unable to enforce her rights as she knew of the mortgage? In *Abbey National Building Society* v *Cann* (6) the defendant claimed an equitable interest in a house purchased by C with the aid of a mortgage. The claim in the House of Lords failed on other grounds but the Court of Appeal held that the defendant's claim failed because she knew that C was going to raise part of the purchase price by a mortgage and therefore had impliedly authorised C to

prior to acquisition or exceptionally at some later date, the court will impose a constructive trust if the party claiming an equitable interest has acted to his detriment or changed his position in reliance on that agreement. If there has been no such agreement, the court relies on conduct to infer the existence of a common intention to share and Lord Bridge doubted whether anything other than a direct contribution to the purchase price would be sufficient to justify the inference. There does not seem to be any express agreement between the parties prior to the acquisition that it would be shared beneficially and Karen has not made any direct contribution to the purchase price, either initially or by contributing to the mortgage repayments. The work which she did in decorating the flat would surely be disregarded as in *Rosset* itself and *Burns* v *Burns* (3).

There is some evidence that at a later stage, John led Karen to believe that she would have a share in the flat as he said to her that he did not put the flat into joint names because of his tax position. This sounds like *Eves* v *Eves* (4) where the man said that the only reason the property was being put in his name alone was that his female partner was under 21, and *Grant* v *Edwards* (5), where the man told his female partner that the only reason the property was not being acquired in joint names was her divorce proceedings. Both ladies acted to their detriment in reliance on this promise and a constructive trust was imposed in their favour. The difficulty for Karen is that John's statement to her was made sometime after the actual acquisition, but Lord Bridge did indicate that in exceptional circumstances a later agreement might be sufficient. He did not give any guidance as to what would constitute exceptional circumstances were. In any event, has Karen acted to her detriment or changed her position in reliance? She has merely continued to live in the flat, although she might argue as in *Greasley* v *Cooke* (6) that she forewent opportunities of moving elsewhere. This does not sound convincing as the period is not so long that it would now be impossible for her to find other accommodation and she has not foregone employment opportunities as in *Greasely* v *Cooke.* She has spent her own money in maintaining and decorating the flat. This might possibly count as acting to her detriment, if done after John's statement to her, but it could be argued that she did this simply in order to be more comfortable. The more money she spent, the more convincing the argument will sound.

On the whole, a claim based on constructive trust to a share in the property does not look very strong. Karen could claim to have a licence to remain in the flat, but the disadvantage of this claim is that it can only give her a right to remain as opposed to a right in the property itself. In *Coombes* v *Smith* (7) the facts were quite similar. The plaintiff claimed a contractual licence on the basis that the defendant had offered to provide a roof over her head if she moved in with him. It was held that there was no enforceable contract. A more attractive claim is one based on proprietary estoppel. Has Karen acted to her detriment in reliance on a mistaken belief in her legal rights? In *Coombes* v *Smith* it was held that the plaintiff had not had a mistaken belief in her legal rights, even though she probably had believed that the defendant would always provide for her. Whenever she had asked for the house to be put into joint names, the defendant had refused and there was no evidence of any discussions about what would happen if the relationship broke down. Karen's case is stronger as John had assured her that she could stay in the flat as long as she wished and that he had left her the flat in his will. It was held in *Re Basham* (8) that proprietary estoppel includes cases where the plaintiff is led to believe that he will have a right in the future.

It is still necessary for Karen to show that she acted to her detriment or altered her position on the faith of her belief. In *Coombes* v *Smith* it was held that having a child, moving away from her husband, redecorating and not trying to provide otherwise for herself did not show acting to one's detriment. The actions were either due simply to a desire to live with the defendant, or done as occupier of the property. By contrast, in *re Basham*, a long history of working without pay, foregoing opportunities to move, caring for the deceased and spending her own money to resolve a boundary dispute were sufficient for a claim based on proprietary estoppel when coupled with frequent promises by the deceased that his property would pass to the plaintiff on his death. Karen's situation looks closer to that in *Coombes* v *Smith*. Although John did promise to leave her the flat in his will, it is difficult to see that Karen has changed her position in reliance on that.

In conclusion therefore Karen could try to claim an interest under a constructive trust or base a claim on proprietary estoppel. The difficulty with the trust claim is that she made no contribution to the acquisition and the only evidence of a common intention that there would be sharing is John's statement made after the purchase. Even if that is enough, Karen must still show that she significantly changed her position as a result and she seems merely to have continued as before. There is no real evidence of contract to found a claim based on contractual licence and the remaining possibility is that of proprietary estoppel. Again Karen's difficulty is that although she was mistaken about her future legal rights, it is not easy to see that she acted to her detriment in reliance. Such acts as looking after a child, failing to provide for herself otherwise and redecorating were held insufficient in *Coombes* v *Smith*. However Karen's claim is not hopeless. In *Coombes* v *Smith* the defendant had already conceded that the plaintiff could stay in the house until the child was 17 and that he would pay the mortgage for that period. It might be that the court would use the flexibility of the doctrine of proprietary estoppel to grant Karen some lesser remedy than a transfer of or share in the flat itself and allow her to remain living there for a limited time until her daughter Clare is, say, 17. There was a clear promise made to her and it is a matter of how flexible the court will be about what constituted acting in reliance on that promise.

References

(1) [1990] 2 WLR 620
(2) [1990] 2 WLR 867
(3) [1984] 1 All ER 244
(4) [1975] 1 WLR 1338
(5) [1986] 3 WLR 114
(6) [1980] 3 All ER 710
(7) [1986] 1 WLR 808
(8) [1986] 1 WLR 1498

QUESTION 6

General Comment

This was probably not a very welcome question to many students as adverse possession is an area of the syllabus which is often omitted in revision and the rules on rectification of the register are sometimes glossed over by those who regard registered land as being solely about overriding interests and in particular s70(1)(g) of the Land Registration Act 1925.

Skeleton Solution

Time period for adverse possession – Aggregation of periods of adverse possession by different owners? – Does the register provide a guarantee of title – Squatters rights or overriding interests? – Compensation for rectification? No loss due to overriding interests not rectification – Position on unregistered land.

Suggested Solution

The Limitation Act 1980 sets a 12 year period for the recovery of land and the issue in this case is to establish whether Henry may still recover possession of the part of his garden on which the tool-shed has been erected, or whether his right of action has been barred by lapse of time since it is more than 12 years since the tool-shed was erected.

The tool-shed was erected on the garden of No 14 in 1975 and time begins to run as soon as the rightful owner has been dispossessed. Adverse possession is a matter of fact, but in this case it seems clear that Peter's acts are inconsistent with Quentin's ownership. Peter had not established title against Quentin when he sold No 12 in 1985, as only ten years had passed, but it is well-established that the period taking the squatter's interest can add the squatter's period of possession to his own. Thus James may aggregate his own and Peter's periods of occupation. There are various situations in which a longer period of occupation is required or when the date from which time begins to run is postponed but there seems no indication that any of these apply in this case.

When he bought No 14 Henry was registered with freehold absolute and the register will show him as the proprietor of the garden including the part with the tool-shed on it. The register is said to provide a state guarantee of title. However this state guarantee is not comprehensive and if James can show that he has acquired title under the Limitation Act, he will be entitled to have the register rectified under s82 Land Registration Act 1925. When Henry purchased No 14 in 1990 he purchased subject to any overriding interests, and rights acquired or in the course of being acquired under the Limitation Acts are overriding interests under s70(1)(f) LRA 1925. Once title has been acquired by adverse possession the registered proprietor holds on trust for the squatter. James may apply for registration as proprietor and will be registered with an absolute or possessory title as appropriate. His estate is a new one and not a transfer of an existing one and will be treated as a first registration.

Although the LRA 1925 does provide for compensation to be paid to any person suffering loss by reason of rectification of the register under s83, it seems that Henry will not be entitled to compensation here. In *Re Chowood* (1) C was registered as proprietor with title absolute to land, but previously L had acquired title to part of that land by adverse possession. The register was rectified against C and C was held not entitled to compensation because C had always bought subject to any overriding interests and C's loss was due not to the rectification but to failing to ascertain the existence of the overriding interest before he purchased. In this case Henry's loss is not due to the rectification but to paying Quentin for land to which Quentin could not make title.

If this were unregistered land James would still be able to claim title by adverse possession but there will be no transfer of title to James from Henry. James's title depends on his possession and the title of Henry is automatically extinguished under s17 Limitation Act 1980.

Reference

(1) [1933] Ch 574

QUESTION 7

General Comment

Most students were probably relieved to find this question on mortgages rather than a problem on priority of mortgages and students with a reasonable knowledge of the relevant case law should have had no difficulty in dealing adequately with this question.

Skeleton Solution

Quotation from *Noakes* v *Rice*: facts – Basic principle: once mortgage paid off, mortgagor should be in same position as before the mortgage – *Bradley* v *Carritt* – Contrast *Kreglinger*: why was the collateral stipulation held binding? – Importance of freedom of contract, don't willingly interfere in businessmen's arrangements – Must be independent bargain – Collateral advantage must not be harsh or unconscionable.

Suggested Solution

The quotation is taken from the case of *Noakes* v *Rice* (1) and the issue raised is that of the validity of collateral advantages in mortgages. The mortgagee may wish to secure some collateral benefit to himself during the mortgage and even wish to secure the continuance of that benefit after the mortgage debt itself has been paid off. The traditional approach of the courts has been to hold that collateral benefits may not continue after redemption of the mortgage, but that approach has been to some extent modified in order to conform to modern business requirements.

In *Noakes* v *Rice* itself, the mortgage included a covenant that the mortgagor would only purchase liquor from the mortgagee and this obligation was expressed to endure even after the redemption of the mortgage. The mortgagor claimed to be able to pay off the mortgage and be free of the covenant and it was held that he should be able to do so. The House of Lords held that whilst a mortgage may provide for a collateral advantage, provided that the collateral advantage was not oppressive or unconscionable and did not clog or fetter the equity of redemption, the collateral advantage must come to an end when the loan was paid off. It was said that a mortgage must not be converted into something else and since the collateral stipulation is part of the mortgage transaction, it must necessarily end with the mortgage. The mortgagor had mortgaged a free house and was entitled to recover a free house and not a tied house when he had repaid the mortgage.

The same principle can be seen in the slightly later decision of *Bradley* v *Carritt* (2). In that case the mortgagor mortgaged his shares which gave him a controlling interest in the company and the mortgage provided that the mortgagor would use his best endeavours to appoint the mortgagee as the company's broker and would pay him the commission the mortgagee would have earned as broker, were he not actually appointed as broker. Some time after the mortgage had been paid off, the shares were sold and the mortgagee lost his appointment as broker. He then sued the mortgagor for his lost commission. It was held that he could not do so as the stipulation was void. It amounted to a clog on the equity of redemption. If it had been valid, it would have been difficult for the mortgagor ever to have sold his shares without rendering himself liable for it was only if he retained his controlling interest in the company that he could ensure that the mortgagee was appointed as broker.

The leading case in which a collateral stipulation was held to remain binding after redemption is *Kreglinger* v *New Patagonia Meat Co* (3). The loan was made on terms that the mortgagee would not call in the principal for five years provided that all interest payments were made on time, but the mortgagor was free to repay within the five years if he wished. The loan was secured by a floating charge and it was provided that the mortgagor would only sell its sheepskins to the mortgagee for a five year period, although the mortgagee agreed to pay the market price for the sheepskins. The loan was repaid within the five year period and the mortgagor claimed to be able to sell its sheepskins to persons other than the mortgagee. It was held that the term was still binding. The House of Lords held that the granting of the collateral advantage was a separate contract independent of the mortgage contract and since it did not amount to a clog on the equity of redemption, it remained valid after the mortgage itself was paid off.

It was true that the mortgagor was still restricted in the conduct of its business after the mortgage was at an end, but the House of Lords was clearly unwilling to intervene in a transaction freely contracted by businessmen, when there had been no inequality of bargaining power and no oppression of the mortgagee. One difference between the *Kreglinger* case and *Bradley* v *Carritt* and *Noakes* v *Rice* is that in *Kreglinger* the collateral advantage was only to last five years from the making of the mortgage. In *Bradley* v *Carritt,* had the collateral advantage remained valid the mortgagor would have been permanently unable to sell his shares, and in *Noakes* v *Rice* the 'tying' was intended to remain effective throughout the duration of the lease of the premises.

Thus broadly Lord Davey's statement remains true but if there is a stipulation in the mortgage which is independent of it, that stipulation may remain binding on the mortgagor after he has repaid the mortgage, even if it does affect the way he may deal with the mortgaged property. There is no doubt that the courts will be less willing to regard such collateral advantages as independent of the mortgage if there is a personal loan than if there is a business transaction between parties of equal bargaining power. The *Kreglinger* doctrine allows the courts a measure of flexibility and perhaps reflects the fact that the mortgagor is not necessarily now the traditional oppressed figure of the last century.

References

(1) [1902] AC 24
(2) [1903] AC 253
(3) [1914] AC 25

QUESTION 8

General Comment

Another fairly standard question on easements which should have caused no problems to most students with a reasonable grasp of the subject. The areas covered included rights capable of existing as easements and acquisition of easements by implied grant.

Skeleton Solution

Does Mick have rights against Rob? – Are storage and the right to play football possible easements? – Four main characteristics of easements – Storage must not amount to exclusive possession – Playing football does not seem to accommodate use of dominant tenement – If rights can be easements, have they been acquired as such – LPA 1925 s62 requirements – Fencing: covenant in lease – Binding on Rob due to s142 LPA and privity of estate – Conclusion: probably Mick can use shed, have fence repaired but not play football.

Suggested Solution

If Mick has a legal right to store his tools and play football on Whiteacre, he will be able to enforce his rights against Rob. If these privileges were merely enjoyed by permission of Pat, Rob will not be bound by them.

Mick will need to show that these rights are capable of existing as easements and that he has acquired them as legal easements. There are four essentials of an easement. There must be a dominant and servient tenement, the easement must accommodate the dominant tenement, the dominant and servient tenements must not be both owned and occupied by the same person and the easement must be capable of forming the subject-matter of a grant. The right of storage was recognised as an easement in *Wright* v *MacAdam* (1), but it is clear from the decisions in *Copeland* v *Greenhalf* (2) and *Grigsby* v *Melville* (3) that if the right claimed is so extensive as to amount to exclusive or joint user of the servient tenement it cannot exist as an easement. It seems that this is a question of degree and further information should be sought on the extent of the right claimed by Mick. It seems unlikely that the right he claims could amount to exclusive or joint user of the shed as he is only storing his tools there, but it may depend on the size of the shed and the number of his tools.

The right to play football is not one of the recognised types of easement. There is a dominant and servient tenement and both are not owned and occupied by the same person. Does the 'easement' accommodate the dominant tenement? In *Hill* v *Tupper* (4) a right to put boats on a canal was not recognised as an easement on the ground that the right was not beneficial to the land itself but merely to Hill's business which he conducted on the land. The right was a personal licence. On the other hand in *re Ellenborough Park* (5) it was held that a right to enjoy a park as a communal garden did accommodate the neighbouring houses. In this case Mick grows vegetables on Blackacre and it is difficult to see that the right to play football on Whiteacre accommodates the use of Blackacre for growing vegetables. If this is wrong it is necessary to consider whether the right is capable of forming the subject-matter of a grant. The nature and extent of the right claimed must be capable of exact description. Again in *re Ellenborough Park* a right to wander at large over the servient tenement was considered sufficiently precise. The list of easements is not closed, but a new category of easement must conform to the four essential characteristics. A new easement is unlikely to be recognised if it would require expenditure by the servient owner, or if it is negative in character – *Phipps* v *Pears* (6). This right does not require expenditure and is not negative, nor does it amount to a claim to joint or exclusive user of Whiteacre. However it is suggested that on balance the right to play football would not be accepted as an easement in this case.

Even if these rights, or some of them, are capable of existing as easements, Mick can only enforce them against Rob, if he has acquired them as legal easements. If the 1988 lease to Mick included an express grant of these rights then the terms of the lease (providing it is a legal and not an equitable lease) will be binding on Rob. If there has been no express grant, Mick will need to rely on implied grant. The right to have the fence kept in repair was contained in the original 1978 lease and may have been repeated in the new lease. Provided that the covenant to keep the fence in good repair was contained in the 1988, as well as in the 1978, lease, Mick as tenant can enforce the covenant against Rob as the assignee of the reversion. There is privity of estate between the parties and the burden of the covenant passes to Rob by LPA 1925 s142 since it has reference to the subject matter of the lease

The other two rights were originally enjoyed by permission only and there is no indication that an express grant was made. It is provided in s62 LPA 1925 that, subject to a contrary intent being expressed, every conveyance of land passes with it 'all liberties, privileges, easements, rights, and advantages whatsoever ... enjoyed with the land'. This section has been held to create easements out of rights previously enjoyed by permission. In *Goldberg* v *Edwards* (7), a right of way enjoyed by revocable licence was turned into an easement by a subsequent grant of a lease. There must be diversity of ownership or occupation for s62 to operate – *Long* v *Gowlett* (8). In this case Mick enjoyed the right to store his tools and play football by permission before the new lease was granted and unless a contrary intention was expressed in the new lease, these rights may have been transformed into easements by s62. However s62 will not apply if the rights claimed cannot exist as easements and if the right to play football cannot exist as an easement at all, it will not become one by virtue of s62.

Thus if these rights can exist as easements and have been acquired as such by Mick either by express or implied grant, Mick may enforce them against Rob. If the right to play football is not an easement, it will be a licence and on these facts it will be a bare licence. The licence will not be binding on Rob. If the right of storage is not an easement, it might be either a lease or a licence. In order to be a lease, there must be exclusive possession, which seems unlikely and there does not seem to be a certain term agreed, nor is it a periodic tenancy as no rent is payable. It is more likely that this right, if not an easement, is a licence and not binding on Rob. It seems likely that the covenant to keep the fence in good repair is part of the lease itself and it will then be binding on Rob.

References

(1) [1949] 2 KB 744
(2) [1952] Ch 488
(3) [1974] 1 WLR 80
(4) (1863) 2 H & C 121
(5) [1956] Ch 131
(6) [1965] 1 QB 76
(7) [1950] Ch 247
(8) [1923] 2 Ch 177

UNIVERSITY OF LONDON
LLB EXAMINATION 1992
PART I
for External Students

LAND LAW

Thursday, 4 June: 10.00am to 1.00pm

Answer *FOUR* of the following EIGHT questions.

1 Distinguish a lease from a licence. To what extent is the distinction important today?

2 Last year Michael inherited a flat in London with 65 years of the lease unexpired. As Michael already had a house of his own in London, he decided to have the flat sold and he left the flat empty pending sale. Subsequently the landlords, Limetree Properties Ltd, sent a section 146 notice to the flat stating that the tenant was in breach of a) the covenant to keep the windows clean, b) the covenant to repaint the front door and the window frames before 1 January 1992 and c) the covenant not to place a window box on the window sill. Michael never saw the notice and two weeks later the landlords peaceably re-entered the flat and changed the locks.

Advise Michael.

3 Alf and Bert own adjoining farms and from January 1972 Alf has used a rough track leading from his farm over Bert's land to the public road. The surface of the track made it only suitable for use by farm vehicles and when the weather was bad, the track was hardly passable at all. Alf and Bert were friends, and Bert never objected to Alf's use of the track. However, in 1990 Alf and Bert quarrelled and when, in April 1991, Alf began work paving the track with a view to making it suitable for passage by all kinds of vehicles, Bert wrote to Alf withdrawing 'the permission I gave you to use the track' and erected a fence barring access to the track from Alf's farm.

Advise Alf.

4 In 1990 Henry bought a house to live in with his girlfriend, Joanna. The house was conveyed into Henry's sole name, but he agreed orally with Joanna that she was to have a 50% beneficial interest in the house. The purchase price was £50,000; Henry provided £5,000 from his savings, Henry's father lent him a further £15,000 and Henry borrowed the remaining £30,000 from the Savewell Bank in whose favour he executed a charge of the property expressed to be by way of legal mortgage. In 1991 Henry lost his job and began to fall badly into arrears with his mortgage repayments. Joanna has now left him and the bank is pressing him to repay his debt even though he is confident that he will find a well paid job within the near future.

Henry would like to know:

a) what his position would be if the bank applied to the court for a possession order;
b) whether he would have any remedy if in the exercise of its power of sale the bank sold the house by private contract for less than its market value; and
c) how the proceeds of sale would be disposed of.

Advise Henry.

5 'The purpose of section 70(1)(g) of the Land Registration Act 1925 was to make applicable to registered land the same rule for the protection of persons in actual occupation of land as had been applied in *Hunt* v *Luck*.'

Explain this statement and consider the extent to which it is accurate.

6 Old Mr Jones, feeling that he would not be able to look after himself for very many more years, wrote to Mary, his unmarried daughter, suggesting that she come and live near him. He offered to buy her a flat to live in. Mary accepted the offer; she gave up her job and her council flat and moved into the flat her father had bought for her. The flat was conveyed into her father's name and he paid the whole of the purchase price. When Mary suggested that she would like the flat to be in her name, he dismissed the idea as absurd because, as he said, 'I am leaving everything to you in my will anyway'. Mr Jones paid all the outgoings on the flat and Mary paid nothing for the use of the flat. Mary found a part-time job and visited her father daily. This arrangement continued happily for two years when Mr Jones died, leaving all his estate to charity. Now his executors seek possession of the flat.

Advise Mary.

Would your advice be any different if Mary had provided one-tenth of the purchase price of the flat?

7 Alan owned Blackacre and the adjoining Whiteacre, and in 1960 he sold Blackacre to Douglas who covenanted with Alan and his successors-in-title a) not to let the property fall into disrepair and b) not to use the property for business purposes.

On the assumption that the land is unregistered, consider how far these covenants will be enforceable:

a) by a lessee of Whiteacre against Douglas;

b) by Alan against an adverse possessor of Blackacre; and

c) by a purchaser of Whiteacre against a purchaser of Blackacre.

8 Mike, Pat, Rob and Saul formed a pop group and decided to buy a house together situated near the recording studios. All four of them contributed equally to the purchase price and the house was conveyed into the joint names of Mike, Pat and Rob; Saul was aged 17 at the time of the conveyance. The pop group was not a success and in 1990 Mike sold his interest in the house to Pat. Shortly afterwards Rob wrote to Pat offering to sell him his interest for a certain price. Pat replied that he would be happy to purchase Rob's interest, but that the price was too high. Before any negotiations took place Rob was killed in a motor accident. Saul now wishes the house to be sold whereas Pat wishes to continue living there.

Saul would like to know whether he can force a sale of the house and, if so, how the proceeds would be divided.

Advise Saul.

QUESTION 1

General Comment

A slight variation on the typical lease/licence question as it is neither solely about *Street* v *Mountford* nor licences as interests in land. The good candidate will cover both these issues in order to answer the question.

Skeleton Solution

Define lease and licence.

Security of tenure.

Exclusive possession.

Street v *Mountford*.

Protection against third party purchasers.

Licence coupled with interest.

Licences and constructive trusts.

Estoppel licences.

Suggested Solution

A lease is a document which creates a term of years in land, in other words it creates an interest in land – a proprietary right. Leases can be legal, ie made by deed in accordance with s52 Law of Property Act (LPA) 1925, or by parol, if they take effect in possession for a term not exceeding three years at the best rent reasonably obtainable (s54 LPA 1925). Licences on the other hand are, generally, merely personal rights giving no interest in land.

The distinction is of fundamental importance in relation to occupancy of residential premises because of the differing degrees of protection afforded to lessees and licencees. In short, lessees are afforded security of tenure whereas licencees are not. If a lease is found to exist the tenant will have the protection of the Protection from Eviction Act 1977, the Rent Act 1977 and the Housing Act 1988. The former governs the periods of notice to quit and the latter two give the tenant valuable rights in terms of security of tenure and the devolution of tenancies. For instance, under both the Rent Act and the Housing Act (with the exception of the assured shorthold tenancy under the latter) a tenant can only be removed from the premises if the landlord can show a mandatory or discretionary ground for possession. Until that time the tenant remains in possession. Similarly, a tenancy can be succeeded to twice under the Rent Act (in favour of a spouse and then members of the tenant's family) and once under the Housing Act. The Rent Act tenant also has valuable rights in relation to rent assessment, whereby rents are subject to review by an adjudication officer.

Licencees on the other hand have no security of tenure, or rent control. They can be removed from the premises following a valid notice to quit, and there is no statutory control of rents. Not surprisingly in the light of the above there has been a continuous battle between landlords, who have constantly tried to create licences out of leases, and tenants who claim the latter. As a result of *Street* v *Mountford* (1), a standard test became applicable in deciding whether an agreement was a lease or not – if the agreement gave the occupant exclusive possession, for a term and at a rent, it was a lease despite any label to the contrary. Subsequent cases have refined that approach and it is now relevant to look not just to the agreement itself but the parties intentions at the time of its making, and how they operated the agreement in practice: *Antoniades* v *Villiers* (2). As a result of these cases certain propositions have emerged. Firstly, in cases of multiple occupancy licences can still exist if there is an absence of the four unities: *AG Securities* v *Vaughan* (2).

Secondly, in exceptional circumstances licences will exist despite the occupant's exclusive possession, eg where the occupant is in possession pursuant to a contract of employment or pending conveyance of the property to him, or pursuant to a local authority's statutory duties. On balance, however, the practice has been to favour the tenant by finding a lease with all its concomitant rights.

The distinction is also important in relation to protection against third parties. A lease is a legal estate in land and if over 21 years and legal, in an area subject to the Land Registration Act 1925, it will be registered as title. If it is legal and under 21 years it will take effect as an overriding interest under s70(1)(k), and is not capable of being overreached. If it is not made by deed and is an equitable lease of any duration, then it can be protected by the entry on the register as a minor interest or, failing that, as an overriding interest under s70(1)(g), although this can be overreached: *City of London Building Society* v *Flegg* (3). By contrast, a licence cannot be protected as title or a minor interest and cannot fall within s70(1)(g) as it is not an interest in land. In the case of land within the ambit of the Land Charges Act 1925, the legal lease will bind 'in rem' and the equitable one can be registered as a C (iv) land charge (estate contract). The licence, on the other hand, has no measure of protection and is not capable of binding third parties.

However, it must not be thought that the licence has no value whatsoever. It has always been recognised that a licence, coupled with an interest or profit, is capable of binding third parties if properly registered. Similarly, some cases of recent origin, eg *Binions* v *Evans* (4), have held that in appropriate cases a purchaser who has knowledge of a contractual licence will be bound by a constructive trust. Others have taken the view that contractual licences have the status of an equity in land (see *Errington* v *Errington* (5), although this was rejected obiter in *Ashburn Anstalt* v *Arnold* (6), where the court preferred the traditional view that contractual licences are personal only: see *King* v *David Allen Billposting* (7).

More importantly, however, estoppel licences have been recognised as giving rise to an interest in land capable of binding third parties. These come about on normal estoppel principles, viz, representation and reliance, and are commonly shown by expenditure on the land of another (*Inwards* v *Baker* (8)), mutual benefit and burden (*Ives* v *High* (9)) and acquiescence (*Plimmer* v *Mayor of Wellington* (10)). In any event once the estoppel has arisen the task for the court is how best to satisfy it. Two of the options open to the court are to grant the licensee a life interest (Inwards) or to convey the fee simple to him (*Pascoe* v *Turner* (11)). Like all estoppels, it will bind everyone except the purchaser for value without notice.

Clearly, in terms of residential occupation in the rented sector, the distinction between a lease and a licence is of fundamental importance. Whereas it might be said that the courts favoured the occupant following *Street* v *Mountford*, the Housing Act has redressed the balance somewhat by the introduction of the assured short-hold tenancy. That said, the licence in other areas is afforded some value, not least through the concept of estoppel.

References

(1) [1985] AC 809
(2) [1988] 3 WLR 1205
(3) [1988] AC 54
(4) [1972] Ch 359
(5) [1952] 1 KB 290
(6) (1987) 2 EGLR 71

References (continued)

(7) [1916] 2 AC 54
(8) [1965] 2 QB 29
(9) [1967] 2 QB 279
(10) (1884) 9 App Cas 699
(11) [1979] 1 WLR 431

QUESTION 2

General Comment

A question which requires some thought and a particular knowledge of the mechanics of s146 notices. Candidates would be expected to deal with the contents of a s146 notice and its service, particularly where one of the covenants requires some repairs. The issue of relief from forfeiture has to be addressed in the light of *Billson* v *Residential Properties*.

Skeleton Solution

Running of leasehold covenants – *Spencer's Case*.

Contents of s146 LPA 1925 notices.

Leasehold Property (Repairs) Act 1938.

Service of s146 notices.

Relief from forfeiture – *Billson* v *Residential Apartments Ltd*.

Suggested Solution

By virtue of his inheritance Michael has obtained a term of years for a period of 65 years, and, as successor in title to the original tenant, he will take the benefit and the burden of all the covenants which touch and concern the land: see *Spencer's Case* (1). Consequently the three covenants, being more than personal covenants, are binding on Michael.

The landlord has served a s146 notice alleging breach of the covenants. It is necessary to see whether that notice is valid. In order for the landlord to forfeit the lease in this manner there must be a forfeiture clause in the lease. I assume that this is the case. According to s146, the notice must include a statement of the breaches, require them to be remedied and compensation. However, the cases have relaxed these requirements in appropriate circumstances.

As required by the section, the notice does specify the breaches complained of. It should have required those breaches to be remedied, but, and as far as the cases go, the notice need only require breaches of positive covenants to be remedied – in this case covenants (a) and (b): see *Scala House and District Properties* v *Forbes*

(2). As regards covenant (c), this is negative in nature, and the view expressed in *Governors of Rugby School* v *Tannahill* (3), was that negative covenants were irremediable and, therefore it was not necessary for the s146 notice to require them to be remedied. In the later case of *Expert Clothing Service and Sales Ltd* v *Hillgate House Ltd* (4), the Court of Appeal suggested that a negative covenant was capable of remedy. If this is correct then the landlord should have required covenant (c) to be remedied – which, after all, would be a comparatively simple task, namely, removing the window box.

If the landlord required compensation in respect of the breaches then he must have specified this in the notice. An additional element must be included in the s146 notice as the Leasehold Property (Repairs) Act 1938 applies, viz, there is a repairing covenant (covenant (b)) in a lease which was originally for a term in excess of seven years and three years remain unexpired. Under the 1938 Act, the s146 notice should have drawn Michael's attention to his rights under the Act.

Assuming that the s146 notice contains the right elements, it is also necessary to look at whether it has been served correctly. Section 146 notices are served by sending them to the lessee or person interested, or by sending them to the demised premises by registered or recorded delivery, or by attaching it to the demised premises. In this case the letter was sent to the flat so, prima facie, that would be good service on Michael. However, as the notice concerns breach of a repairing covenant s18 Landlord and Tenant Act 1927 should have been complied with. Section 18 requires that service of the notice must be *known* to the lessee, under-lessee or the person who last paid rent. In our case Michael (the new lessee) did not know of the notice and therefore it is invalid.

Insofar as the landlord purported to re-enter pursuant to the notice several points have to be made. Firstly, s18 Landlord and Tenant Act 1927 states that reasonable interval must have elapsed between the date on which service was known to the appropriate person and the actual re-entry. Whether two weeks would be reasonable is a moot point even if it could be shown that Michael knew of the notice. Secondly, and more importantly, it is now settled as a result of the House of Lords' judgment in *Billson* v *Residential Apartments Ltd* (5), that a tenant can apply for relief from forfeiture under s146(2) whenever a landlord *has* re-entered pursuant to a s146 notice but without a court order – as is the case here. Therefore, following *Billson* it would be open to Michael to apply for relief against forfeiture.

In deciding whether to grant relief, the court will look at the gravity of the breach and all the circumstances of the case in order to see whether it is just and equitable to do so. On the facts breaches of covenants (a) and (c) are of a trivial nature, and whereas covenant (b) is not so trivial, it is not in the nature of breach of a user or assignment covenant. In the circumstances it is quite possible that the court will grant relief, and in doing so it can attach conditions, eg that Michael pay all, or part, of the landlord's expenses.

References

(1) (1583) 5 Co Rep 16
(2) [1974] QB 575
(3) [1935] 1 KB 87
(4) [1986] Ch 340
(5) [1992] 1 All ER 141

QUESTION 3

General Comment

Not a particularly difficult question on easements. The key issues to deal with are whether there is permission or acquiescence on the part of Bert, whether the limited time during which the path was useable is relevant and whether Alf can improve the path. Candidates who are aware of *Mills* v *Silver* should not be unduly troubled by this question.

Skeleton Solution

Definition of easement.

Characteristics of easement – *Re Ellenborough Park.*

Acquisition of easements generally.

Prescription – acquiescence or permission – *Dalton* v *Angus* – nec vi, nec clam, nec precario – Prescription Act 1832 – 20 years' user – *Mills* v *Silver.*

Maintenance or improvement of easements – *Mills* v *Silver.*

Suggested Solution

An easement is a right in or over the land of another – it is a right 'in alieno solo'. Alf wishes to know whether he can continue to make use of the track across Bert's land. In order to be able to do so he must show that the track has the characteristics of an easement, and has been acquired as such.

The characteristics of an easement were laid down in *Re Ellenborough Park* (1) as follows. Firstly, there must be a dominant and servient tenement. The dominant tenement has the benefit of the alleged easement and the servient the burden. In this case Alf's farm is the dominant tenement and Bert's the servient.

Secondly, the easement must 'accommodate' the dominant tenement. In *Re Ellenborough Park* the court said that an easement would do so if it made the dominant tenement a 'better and more convenient property', eg if it increased the value of that property. It was also said in that case that there must be a sufficient nexus between the enjoyment of the easement and the dominant tenement; in other words the servient and dominant tenements must be proximate, but not necessary adjoining or adjacent, so as to enable the dominant tenement to derive a realistic benefit from the easement. On the facts it is clear that the nexus test is satisfied as the farms are adjoining, and it could also be argued that the use of a path over Bert's land increases the value of Alf's farm. In addition it must be shown that the easement accommodates the land (Alf's farm) as opposed to the person (Alf), as an easement is more than a mere personal right: see *Hill* v *Tupper* (2) and *Moody* v *Steggles* (3). As paths are the most common type of easement it may be safe to assume that the easement accommodates the land.

Thirdly, the dominant and servient land must be owned and occupied by different persons. This is clearly satisfied as Bert owns the servient land and Alf the dominant. Finally, the easement must be capable of forming the subject matter of grant – it must be a right which could have been granted by deed. For this to be satisfied there must be a capable grantor and grantee, and as there is nothing to suggest that Bert or Alf are subject to some incapacity at law there would be a grantor and grantee respectively. The right claimed as an easement also needs to be sufficiently definite and not a claim of privacy or view, as well as being in the nature of a recognised easement. Again these requirements are satisfied as a path in the nature of a right of way is one of the oldest recognised easements.

Thus the path across Bert's land is capable of being an easement in the form of a right of way in favour of Alf. However, whether Alf actually has an easement depends on whether he has acquired it in a manner recognised by law.

An easement can be acquired in several ways, most of which can be discounted here. There is no suggestion of an express grant of an easement by Bert in favour of Alf, nor is there likely to be an easement of necessity in the absence of Alf's farm being 'land-locked': see *Wong* v *Beaumont* (4) and *Nickerson* v *Barraclough* (5). Similarly, in the absence of a conveyance between Bert and Alf, s62 Law of Property Act 1925 and the doctrine in *Wheeldon* v *Burrows* (6) cannot apply. Therefore, if Alf has acquired an easement at all he will have done so by prescription.

A prescriptive easement can be acquired in three ways – common law prescription, lost modern grant, and under the Prescription Act 1832. All three are based on acquiescence and it is necessary to show that the servient owner knows of the use over his land by the dominant owner, has the power to stop it or sue in respect of it, and fails to do: *Dalton* v *Angus* (7). On the facts it would appear that these factors are satisfied as Bert knows of Alf's use of the track and only takes steps to stop it in 1991. All three types of prescription are also based on longer user as of right, without force, secrecy or permission (nec vi, nec clam, nec precario). These factors will now be considered in respect of the different types of prescription.

In order to successfully plead common law prescription, Alf would have to show that the path has been used across Bert's farm since time immemorial – 1189. Although the rule is deemed to be satisfied if the use can be shown to have existed throughout the memory of the oldest living inhabitant of the area, such a plea will fail even if the farms had existed since that time in view of the fact that the path has, apparently, only existed since 1972. Alf may have more success in pleading lost modern grant. This is essentially a fiction whereby 20 years' user or more as of right was presumed to arise from the grant of a deed which had since been lost: *Tehidy Minerals* v *Norman* (8). The difficulty for Alf here would be that he could not show 20 years' user as of right. Obviously until April 1991 there is 19 years and four months' user as of right, but since then user has been prevented by virtue of the fence across the path.

Alf's strongest case lies in pleading the Prescription Act 1832. Under s2 and s4 of the Act, 20 years' user as of right next before some suit or action without interruption must be shown. Several points must be considered here: is there 20 years' user in view of the fact that the path is not passable when the weather is bad?; has Alf used as of right?; and is there an interruption?

As to the first point, it was settled in *Mills* v *Silver* (9) that an easement in the form of right of way could come into existence notwithstanding the fact that the path in question could only be used in dry weather. As to the second point, Bert will no doubt seek to argue that he had given Alf permission to use the path back in January 1972 as indicated in his letter of April 1991; however, a distinction must be drawn between acquiescence which is the basis of prescription (*Dalton* v *Angus*) and permission. If there was true permission Alf cannot claim an easement, but if there was acquiescence or toleration it is not open for Bert to seek to grant permission ex post facto by his letter of April 1991.

The 20-year period can, of course, be defeated by an interruption provided that it lasts for at least one year and is known to the dominant owner who submits to it. Although it is reasonable to assume Alf knows of the existence of the fence, it is not clear whether he has submitted to it. In any event it will not be a valid interruption because the year of interruption will expire in April 1992, whereas the 20 years' user will expire four months earlier in January 1992, thereby enabling Alf to claim the easement.

Hence, Alf appears to have acquired a legal easement over

Bert's farm by virtue of the Prescription Act 1832, which will entitle him to get a mandatory injunction requiring Bert to remove the fence. However, the easement is limited to the right to pass and re-pass along the track. In other words it does not give Alf the right to improve the track, merely to repair it, and insofar as Alf has commenced improvements by paving the track he has committed a trespass which will enable Bert to recover damages from him (see *Mills* v *Silver*).

References

(1) [1956] Ch 131
(2) (1863) 2 H & C 121
(3) (1879) LR 12 Ch D 261
(4) [1965] 1 QB 173
(5) [1980] Ch 325
(6) (1879) 12 Ch D 31
(7) (1881) 6 App Cas 740
(8) [1971] 2 QB 528
(9) [1991] 2 WLR 324

QUESTION 4

General Comment

A question which coupled the law of mortgages and trusts. As regards the bank seeking possession mention must be made of the Administration of Justice Acts. The case of *Cuckmere Brick* must be discussed in the context of the low sale price, and s105 Law of Property Act (LPA) 1925 as regards the distribution of proceeds. In dealing with the distribution of proceeds it is necessary to see whether Henry's father and Joanna can claim an interest in the house, and, consequently, in the proceeds. Constructive trusts, resulting trusts and proprietary estoppel should be considered in this context.

Skeleton Solution

Definition of mortgage.

Four Maids v *Dudley Marshall*.

Possession a prelude to sale – dwelling house – s36 Administration of Justice Act 1970 – s8 Administration of Justice Act 1973.

Cuckmere Brick Co Ltd v *Mutual Finance Ltd* – mortgagee's duty of care on sale – negligence.

Section 101 LPA 1925 – s103 LPA 1925 – distribution of proceeds: s105 LPA 1925.

Interest for father – loan – *Re Sharpe*.

Interest for Joanna – constructive or resulting trust.

Suggested Solution

A mortgage is a security for a loan and can be either legal or equitable. In this case Savewell Bank have a legal mortgage in the form of a charge over the property. As legal mortgagee the bank have certain powers, namely of sale, to take possession, to foreclose and to appoint a receiver.

a) *Possession*

The bank are entitled to take possession of the house 'before the ink is dry on the mortgage' (*Four Maids* v *Dudley Marshall* (1)), unless they have expressly or impliedly excluded their right to do so (*Birmingham Citizens' Permament Building Society* v *Caunt* (2)). Should the bank wish to rely on these broad rights, possession will only be granted if it is equitable to do so: *Quennell* v *Maltby* (3). In reality however, possession is usually sought for two different reasons. Firstly, if the mortgagee does not wish to realise his security he may seek possession of the land with a view to intercepting the rents and profits from the land, and recovering his interest. Such a move is attended by liability on the basis of wilful default, in the sense that the mortgagee will be liable to the mortgagor not for the income he actually generates from the land, but for the income he could have generated from the land: *White* v *City of London Brewery* (4).

The second use of possession is as a prelude to sale, as the mortgagee will wish to obtain possession in order to sell with vacant possession. This appears to be the case here. In these circumstances there are several remedies open to Henry as the action concerns a dwelling house. Under s36 Administration of Justice Act 1970, the court may adjourn or suspend or postpone proceedings if the mortgagor could, within a reasonable time, pay off the arrears. The fact that Henry is confident that he will find a well paid job in the near future is a relevant consideration. On the assumption that the mortgage is an instalment mortgage, the court may treat as the sums owing only those instalments which are actually in arrear, even though the mortgage may require the whole of the outstanding balance to be paid upon default: s8 Administration of Justice Act 1973.

In the circumstances then it would be open to Henry to apply to the court under the Administration of Justice Act 1970 to postpone or suspend any order for possession sought by the bank.

b) *Sale at less than market value*

In the first place the bank, as mortgagee, has an absolute discretion as to the mode and time of sale. It can choose to sell by way of private treaty (as in this case) or by way of auction, and it is not obliged to wait until the market improves. However, once the bank decides to sell it is subject to certain duties. First, and foremost, it is clear from *Cuckmere Brick Co Ltd* v *Mutual Finance Ltd* (5) that a mortgagee is not a trustee for the mortgagor in respect of the power of sale. He is, however, a trustee in respect of how that power is exercised and accordingly owes a duty of care to the mortgagor or guarantor to obtain the best price upon sale: *Standard Chartered Bank* v *Walker* (6). Failure to do so will render the mortgagee liable to the mortgagor for the difference between the price he obtained and the price he could have obtained (*Cuckmere*).

c) *Proceeds of sale*

As the mortgage is by way of legal charge made by deed after 1881, the power of sale has arisen in favour of the bank (s101 LPA 1925), and in view of the fact that Henry is badly in arrear, one of the conditions making the power exercisable under s103 LPA 1925 has been satisfied. Upon sale being concluded the proceeds of sale will be distributed in accordance with s105 LPA 1925. Under that section, in the absence of any prior encumbrance, the costs and expenses of sale will be defrayed first, then the bank will take the mortgage monies owing to it, any balance will be paid to subsequent mortgagees if any, and if not, to the mortgagor (Henry). Should there be any prior encumbrances they will be paid first.

Assuming the proceeds of sale are sufficient to satisfy the mortgage debt and leave a balance, that balance is paid to the mortgagor (Henry). The question is whether Henry's father and Joanna are entitled to a share of that balance.

It is likely that the father will be entitled to a share in the balance by virtue of the loan he made to Henry. As it is a loan, it negatives any presumption of advancement or gift between father and son, and, according to *Re Sharpe* (7) and *Hussey* v *Palmer* (8), would give the father an interest in property pending repayment of the loan. In the circumstances Henry's father will be entitled to the repayment of his £15,000 loan.

On the other hand it is unlikely that Joanna will be able to claim a share in the proceeds. In the first place she has not made any direct financial contribution to the purchase of the house either by way of deposit or mortgage instalments, so as to establish a beneficial interest in her favour under a resulting or constructive trust (*Lloyds Bank* v *Rosset* (9)). Secondly, although she may be able to point to the oral agreement that she should have 50 per cent share in the house, she does not appear to have acted to her detriment upon that agreement so as to raise an interest under a trust or by way of estoppel in her favour: *Lloyds Bank* v *Rosset* and *Grant* v *Edwards* (10).

References

(1) [1957] Ch 317
(2) [1962] Ch 883
(3) [1979] 1 WLR 318
(4) (1889) 42 Ch D 327

References (continued)

(5) [1971] Ch 949
(6) [1982] 1 WLR 144
(7) [1980] 1 WLR 219
(8) [1972] 1 WLR 1286
(9) [1990] 2 WLR 867
(10) [1986] Ch 638

QUESTION 5

General Comment

A question which requires candidates to state what the rule in *Hunt* v *Luck* is, how it applies and then to compare it with s70(1)(g). The similarities and the differences between the two principles should be teased out. This is not a question for the student who either does not know what *Hunt* v *Luck* says or is unable to analyse it.

Skeleton Solution

Explanation of *Hunt* v *Luck* – explanation of doctrine of notice.

Elements of s70(1)(g) LRA 1925.

Need to investigate the land.

Enquiries of persons on the land.

Overreaching.

Suggested Solution

The rule in *Hunt* v *Luck* (1) is intimately connected with the common law doctrine of notice. At common law the purchaser of land was bound by any equitable interest in land of which he had actual, constructive or imputed notice. The rule in *Hunt* can be expressed as follows; a purchaser of land must make enquiries of any person in possession of the land and if he fails to do so then any title he acquires will be subject to that of the person in possession. In short, the purchaser would be caught by constructive notice. In its original formulation the rule was only applicable to the interests of a tenant in possession, but was later extended to cover the interests of any person in possession.

Section 70(1)(g) applies in the context of the Land Registration Act 1925 and is one of the categories of overriding interest. As such it will not appear on the land certificate thereby shattering the 'mirror principle', and, as an overriding interest it is capable of binding a purchaser. In order for s70(1)(g) to be made out a person must be in actual occupation of the land (see *Epps* v *Esso Petroleum Co Ltd* (2)) with an interest in land capable of binding subsequent owners of the land, in other words, a proprietary interest as opposed to a personal one (*Williams & Glyn's Bank* v *Boland* (3)).

Additionally he must not have concealed that interest upon enquiry being made of him.

In *Strand Securities* v *Caswell* (4), Lord Denning described s70(1)(g) as carrying the rule in *Hunt* forward into registered land. Insofar as the person in actual occupation must have an interest in land, s70(1)(g) and *Hunt* are the same. Similarly both recognise that the presence of the vendor on the land does not exclude the possibility of occupation by another. In *Hunt* the occupation was that of the lessee, in *Boland* it was that of the wife although Lord Wilberforce said that the rule could apply in favour of any person in actual occupation.

However, there are marked differences. Whereas *Hunt* is based on, and requires some investigation of the land, s70(1)(g) will bind a purchaser whether he knows of the existence of the right or not and whether he could have discovered it or not; it does not require any search or investigation of the land and is not in any way based on the doctrine of notice.

Secondly, like *Hunt*, if enquiry is made under s70(1)(g) and the rights are not disclosed (as a result of active concealment on the part of the person who claims them), the purchaser will take free of them. But, unlike *Hunt*, s70(1)(g) neither requires nor presupposes any enquiry being made in the first place.

Thirdly, unlike *Hunt*, the overriding interests of a person in actual occupation of land under s70(1)(g) can be overreached by a purchaser. In order to do so the purchaser must comply with the provisions of s2 LPA 1925, viz, he must take a conveyance from trustees, the interest must be of a type which is capable of being overreached and he must pay the capital monies to two trustees or a trust corporation: see *City of London Building Society* v *Flegg* (5) and contrast *Boland*. The fact that s70(1)(g) is capable of being overreached serves to highlight the fact that a search or investigation of the land is not pre-supposed for the purposes of that section.

Fourthly, s70(1)(g) protects not just the person in actual occupation but also the recipient of rents and profits from the land. In this respect it is wider than the rule in *Hunt*.

Therefore there is limited truth in the statement. Both *Hunt* and s70(1)(g) deal with the interests of a person in occupation, but the former is rooted in the doctrine of notice – the latter is not and is capable of being avoided by way of overreaching.

References

(1) [1901] 1 Ch 45
(2) [1973] 1 WLR 1071
(3) [1981] AC 487
(4) [1965] Ch 958
(5) [1988] AC 54

QUESTION 6

General Comment

A question involving the acquisition of a beneficial interest in land. A good knowledge of resulting and constructive trusts and the principles of proprietary estoppel is needed. Candidates attempting this question should be able to demonstrate a good grasp of the relevant principles and authorities, and the ability to apply them to the facts. It is important to structure the answer in a logical and coherent fashion.

Skeleton Solution

Declaration of trust in conveyance – *Goodman* v *Gallant*.

Constructive or resulting trusts – express informal agreement – *Eves* v *Eves* and *Cooke* v *Head* – direct financial contributions.

Proprietary estoppel – *Lloyds Bank* v *Rosset; Re Basham* and *Grant* v *Edwards*.

Suggested Solution

In order for Mary to claim an interest in the flat she will have to look to equity for assistance. Mary is not on the title deeds so no trust arises in her favour as in *Goodman* v *Gallant* (1). Consequently, the law relating to resulting and constructive trusts and proprietary estoppel must be considered.

In the first place it is notable that Mary has not made any direct financial contributions to the purchase of the flat, whether by way of deposit or instalments. Her father provided all the purchase monies and therefore Mary cannot claim an interest based on an imputed intention that she should have an interest: see Lord Bridge in *Lloyds Bank* v *Rosset* (2).

Mary could seek to argue that she has an interest by virtue of express informal agreement at the date of acquisition (or exceptionally later) with her father, which she has acted upon to her detriment (see Lord Bridge in Rosset). It is unclear whether the father made the statement at the time of buying the flat or later, but it may be possible to assert that his response to Mary's request to put the property into her name ('I'm leaving everything to you anyway') is evidence of such an agreement as was recognised in *Cooke* v *Head* (3) and *Eves* v *Eves* (4). In the former case the man said that the woman's name should not appear on the title deeds as it might prejudice her pending divorce, and in the latter because she was too young. In both cases the Court of Appeal took the view that the statements were evidence of an intention that the women should have an interest. If Cooke and Eves are followed, Mary will have an interest which is determined according to the agreement and not in proportion to any contribution she may have made.

In order to succeed in such a plea Mary would have to establish not only the existence of the agreement but also that she acted to her detriment on it. The most common form of detriment is a material sacrifice in the nature of financial contributions or improvements to property. On the facts Mary has not acted to her detriment in either of these ways and it is a moot point whether she has acted to her detriment in giving up her job and council flat, so as to raise a constructive trust in her favour. It could be argued that the giving up of the council flat is connected with the alleged agreement (*Grant* v *Edwards* (5)) but, the giving up of the job may not be related to the agreement at all but may have been the result of Mary's love and affection for her father.

Should Mary fail to establish an interest under a constructive trust she may be able to rely on a proprietary estoppel – a point which was specifically recognised by Lord Bridge in Rosset where he approved *Grant* and *Re Basham* (6). Mary would have to show that there was a representation that she would receive an interest, then or in the future: *Re Basham*. For these purposes her father's statement would suffice. Additionally, Mary would have to show that she acted to her detriment in reliance on that statement. Therefore, the date when the statement was made is all important. Assuming that the statement preceded Mary leaving her flat and job, those acts could be seen as acts of detriment: see *Jones* v *Jones* (7). Mary's acts of visiting her father are likely to be seen as the acts of a loving and caring daughter and not acts of detriment. Should the father's statement have come after Mary gave up her job and flat, those acts cannot be seen as acts *in reliance on* that statement, and an estoppel will not arise.

On balance, it seems unlikely that Mary can plead that a resulting or constructive trust has arisen in her favour, but it may be possible for her to show that an estoppel has arisen which binds everyone except the bona fide purchaser: *Inwards* v *Baker* (8).

If Mary had provided one-tenth of the purchase price

If Mary had provided one-tenth of the purchase price, in the absence of evidence to show that it was a gift to her father, she would acquire an interest in the property, proportionate to her contribution, by virtue of a resulting trust by way of direct financial contribution referable to acquisition.

References

(1) [1986] Fam 106
(2) [1990] 2 WLR 867
(3) [1972] 1 WLR 518
(4) [1975] 1 WLR 1338
(5) [1986] Ch 638
(6) [1986] 1 WLR 1498
(7) [1977] 1 WLR 438
(8) [1965] 2 QB 29

QUESTION 7

General Comment

Not a difficult question for the candidate who is well-prepared. An understanding of how covenants affect successors-in-title other than purchasers is essential. The principles of registration must also be considered.

Skeleton Solution

Definition of restrictive covenant.

Running of benefit to covenantee's successor – common law rules – *Smith & Snipes Hall Farm* v *River Douglas Catchment Board* – s78 LPA 1925.

Limitation Act 1980.

Re Nisbet & Potts' Contract – annexation – *Mill Lodge Properties Ltd.*

Running of benefit to covenantee's successor in equity – annexation – assignment – building scheme.

Running of burden to covenantor's successor – *Tulk* v *Moxhay.*

Registration.
Section 84 LPA 1925.

Suggested Solution

A restrictive covenant is an agreement under seal whereby one party (the covenantor) agrees with another party (the covenantee) that he (the covenantor) will, or will not, do certain acts in relation to a defined area of land. The land owned by the covenantee will have the benefit of the covenant and that owned by the covenantor will have the burden. On the facts Alan, who owns Whiteacre, is the covenantee and Douglas, who owns Blackacre, is the covenantor.

Covenant (a) is a positive covenant because it requires the covenantor, or his successors, to maintain and repair Blackacre. Covenant (b) is negative in that it simply prohibits the use of Blackacre for business purposes.

a) *Lessee of Whiteacre*

A lessee of Whiteacre would be a successor-in-title to the original covenantee (Alan). In order to be able to enforce the covenants against Douglas (the original covenantor) the lessee must have obtained the benefit of the covenants. This he can do under the common law rules governing the running of the benefit. At common law four conditions have to be complied with in order for the benefit to run. Firstly, the covenants must 'touch and concern' the land. In *Smith & Snipes Hall Farm* v *River Douglas Catchment Board* (1) this was said to be satisfied if the covenants affected mode of occupation, or directly affected the value of land. Covenant (b) clearly affects mode of occupation and (a) affects value. Secondly, the original covenantee must have had a legal estate in land. In this case Alan did have a legal estate in Whiteacre, presumably in the nature of fee simple.

Thirdly, the successor to the covenantee must have a legal estate in land, although not necessarily the same legal estate. This is also satisfied because the lessee would have a legal term of years in the land. In any event this requirement has been abrogated by s78 Law of Property Act (LPA) 1925 which states that a covenant relating to land of the covenantee shall be deemed to be made with the covenantee *and his successors-in-title and the persons deriving title under him or them,* and so extends to a lessee of the covenantee. Fourthly, there must be an intention that the covenants should run with the land. This too is covered by s78 which provides that such an intention is deemed to be present and does not admit of a contrary intention.

If the conditions are satisfied the benefit of both the positive covenant (a) and the negative one (b), will have run to the lessee enabling him to enforce them against Douglas.

It should be noted that it is not necessary to show that the burden of the covenants has run to Douglas as he is the original covenantor. Neither is it necessary to deal with registration because that would only be relevant when dealing with a purchaser of the burdened land (Blackacre).

b) *Adverse possessor of Blackacre*

An adverse possessor of Blackacre will have obtained Blackacre under the Limitation Act 1980, by showing 12 years' possession adverse to the paper owner (Douglas). In running up that time the adverse possessor must show factual possession and the intention to possess.

As the adverse possessor is not a purchaser of the servient

land (Blackacre) he will be bound by any covenants which are annexed to the land: *Re Nisbet & Potts' Contract* (2). This applies to both positive and negative covenants whether they are registered as D(ii) land charges or not. The covenants could be shown to be annexed in two ways, firstly, by way of express annexation and, secondly, by virtue of s78.

Express annexation will occur if certain conditions are satisfied. It must be possible to identify the land to be benefited from the wording of the covenants. In *Rogers* v *Hosegood* (3) the covenant was deemed to be annexed as it referred to the dominant land; however, in *Renals* v *Cowlishaw* (4) the covenant was not annexed because it referred solely to 'heirs, executors, administrators and assigns'. It is not clear from the limited facts whether the dominant land is capable of being identified from the covenants themselves. Where the dominant land is sold off in plots it is also necessary to show that the covenants were annexed to each and every part of the estate rather than to the estate as a whole: *Re Selwyn's Conveyance* (5). This is not the case here. It would also appear from *Re Ballard's Conveyance* (6), that annexation can only occur where substantially the whole of the dominant land is capable of benefitting. There is nothing to suggest that Whiteacre is so large as to prevent this happening.

Alternatively, s78 LPA could operate to annex the covenants to the land. In *Federated Homes* v *Mill Lodge Properties Ltd* (7) the court held that a covenant could be annexed to land by virtue of the section where the dominant land was identifiable and the covenants touched and concerned the land as per *Smith & Snipes*.

Consequently, provided there is effective annexation, Alan, the original covenantee, can enforce both covenants against the adverse possessor of Blackacre.

c) *A purchaser of Whiteacre and a purchaser of Blackacre*

In order for a purchaser of Whiteacre from Alan to enforce the covenants against a purchaser of Blackacre from Douglas, it must be shown that the benefit of the covenants has run to the former and the burden to the latter.

The purchaser of Whiteacre will be a successor-in-title to the covenantee, and the benefit of the covenants could run to him at common law or equity. The running of the benefit at common law has been dealt with in part a) above. This is not likely to be a successful way of enforcing the covenant as, with very limited exceptions (eg chain of indemnity covenants, long leases), the burden of covenants does not run at common law.

Consequently, it will be better for the purchaser to show that benefit and burden have run in equity. The benefit of the covenants can run in equity in four different ways, namely, annexation, assignment, building scheme and under s78 LPA 1925.

Annexation and s78 have already been dealt with under part b) above. Assignment is the process of transferring the benefit of the covenant to the covenantee's successor. In order for this to be achieved it has to be shown that the dominant land (Whiteacre) can be identified, directly or indirectly, in the assignment (see *Newton Abbot Co-operative Society* v *Williamson & Treadgold* (8)), secondly, that the assignment was contemporaneous with transfer or conveyance, and thirdly, that there was a clear intention to assign.

A building scheme or scheme of development is governed by the rules laid down in *Elliston* v *Reacher* (9), as amended: see *Re Dolphin's Conveyance* (10) and *Baxter* v *Four Oaks Properties Ltd* (11). Those rules require an intention on the part of the vendor to set up a building scheme in relation to a defined area of land. As long as that intention is manifest, the purchasers buy subject to the scheme of covenants which crystallises upon the first purchase. Under the scheme each purchaser can enforce, and have enforced against him, the negative covenants which make up the scheme.

Provided one of the four methods discussed above can be satisfied, the benefit of the covenants will have run to the purchaser of Whiteacre in equity.

The running of the burden of the covenants to the purchaser of Blackacre in equity is governed by the rule in *Tulk* v *Moxhay* (12). Under *Tulk* four conditions have to be satisfied. Firstly, the covenants must touch and concern the land as per *Smith & Snipes* (discussed above). Secondly, the covenants must be negative in substance. Equity will not enforce positive covenants against a successor-in-title to the covenantor. The test to determine whether a covenant is negative is the 'hand in pocket test': *Haywood* v *Brunswick Permanent Benefit Building Society* (13). If the covenant requires the covenantor to expend money it is positive and cannot be enforced against a successor-in-title. On the facts covenant (a) is positive and cannot be enforced against the purchaser of Blackacre from Douglas.

Thirdly, at the time the covenant was made the original covenantee must have retained land capable of benefitting from it. On the facts when the covenant was made in 1960 Alan, the original covenantee, retained land capable of benefiting

(Whiteacre). Fourthly, there must have been an intention that the burden should run. This is provided for by s79 LPA 1925; in the absence of contrary intention the covenantor is deemed to covenant on behalf of himself and successors.

If these four factors are present the burden of covenant (b) will have run to the purchaser of Blackacre in equity. However, it is not enough to show that benefit and burden have run in equity – in order to be enforceable against the purchaser of Blackacre it must be shown that covenant (b) was properly protected by the registration of a D(ii) land charge by Alan (the original covenantee), against the name of Douglas (the original covenantor). If it was, the purchaser of Blackacre will be bound by it; if not, he will take free of it: see *Midland Bank* v *Green* (14).

Even if benefit and burden have run in equity and covenant (b) was registered as a D(ii) charge, the purchaser of Blackacre may be able to rely on s84 LPA 1925 to modify or discharge the covenant. This can be done if he can show one of the following grounds: that the covenant is obsolete due to changes in the character of the neighbourhood, that it impedes the reasonable development of land, that it could be discharged without adversely affecting the covenantee or his successors, or there is agreement to do so.

References

(1) [1949] 2 KB 500
(2) [1905] 1 Ch 391
(3) [1900] 2 Ch 388
(4) (1878) 9 Ch D 125
(5) [1967] Ch 674
(6) [1937] Ch 473
(7) [1980] 1 WLR 594
(8) [1952] Ch 286
(9) [1908] 2 Ch 374
(10) [1970] Ch 654
(11) [1965] Ch 816
(12) (1848) 2 Ph 774
(13) (1881) 8 QBD 403
(14) [1981] 2 WLR 28

QUESTION 8

General Comment

A fairly straightforward question on severance of a joint tenancy and the operation of s30 LPA 1925. The only 'tricky' part lies in the fact that one joint tenant sells to another, so that that other remains a joint tenant of his original share and becomes a tenant-in-common in respect of his 'new share'.

Skeleton Solution

Co-ownership trust for sale – s34–36 LPA 1925.

Joint tenancy – four unities – contributions.

Severance – *Williams* v *Hensman*.

Sale to existing joint tenant – *Re Mayo*.

Section 30 LPA 1925 application for order for sale – secondary or collateral trusts – *Jones* v *Challenger*.

Suggested Solution

Whenever two or more people contribute to the purchase of property which is not conveyed into all of their names, the Law of Property Act (LPA) 1925 brings into play a trust for sale in favour of the co-owners.

Mike, Pat, Rob and Saul contribute equally to the purchase of the house, and they are thus co-owners. As Saul is a minor he cannot hold the legal estate (s1(6) LPA 1925), and so the house is conveyed into the names of Mike, Pat and Rob who hold it on trust for sale for themselves and Saul in equity (ss34–36 LPA 1925). The legal estate is held by the three of them as joint tenants as a tenancy-in-common cannot exist at law.

All four hold the equitable interests as joint tenants for the following reasons. Firstly, the four unities (possession, interest, time and title) appear to be present as all of them are entitled to possess and occupy the house, all of them have the same interest (presumably fee simple), they all acquired that interest at the same time, namely, the date of conveyance, and they all acquired it under the same act or document, viz, the purchase of the house. Secondly, they have contributed equally to the purchase in which case equity presumes a joint tenancy. Thirdly, the house is purchased to be lived in, it is not purchased as a business asset or as business premises (see *Malayan Credit* v *Jack Chia* (1)), although it will enable them to get to the recording studio easier.

As they are joint tenants none of them can point to a specific share of the property as being theirs – they each own the entirety, although upon sale they will each be entitled to a quarter share of the proceeds. Moreover, as there is a joint tenancy the doctrine of survivorship operates so that, unless a joint tenant has severed his interest during life, his interest passes to the other joint tenants on his death.

The interests of the four could be expressed as follows:

Mike	Pat	Rob		Legal Title (Joint Tenants)
Mike	Pat	Rob	Saul	Equity
JT	JT	JT	JT	
$\frac{1}{4}$	$\frac{1}{4}$	$\frac{1}{4}$	$\frac{1}{4}$	

A joint tenancy can be severed by a joint tenant acting upon his 'share', eg by selling it. In fact the tenancy will have been severed the moment Mike entered into a specifically enforceable contract of sale with Pat. The transaction has no effect on the legal title and Mike remains a trustee for sale. As far as the equitable interests are concerned, Mike drops out of the picture and is no longer a beneficiary behind the trust for sale. Pat will remain a joint tenant in equity of his original interest vis-a-vis Rob and Saul, and will have become a tenant-in-common in respect of the share he has acquired from Mike. He cannot be a joint tenant in respect of this share because unity of title is missing.

The interests of the parties can now be expressed as follows:

Mike	Pat	Rob		Legal Title (Joint Tenants)
Mike	Pat	Rob	Saul	Equity
(TIC)	JT	JT	JT	
$(\frac{1}{4})$	$\frac{1}{4}$	$\frac{1}{4}$	$\frac{1}{4}$	

Although a joint tenancy can be severed by way of mutual agreement or mutual conduct (see *Williams* v *Hensman* (2), neither could be said to have occurred here, as the price had not been agreed (contrast: *Burgess* v *Rawnsley* (3)). The letter then has no effect on either the legal or beneficial interests.

Rob's death does not effect a severance of his interest in the house, but rather survivorship operates and his share passes to the two remaining joint tenants, Pat and Saul. The legal estate is now vested in Mike and Pat as trustees for sale on trust for Saul and Pat as joint tenants of their original shares and the share of Rob which has passed to them by survivorship, and Pat as tenant-in-common in respect of the share he purchased from Mike, viz:

Mike	Pat		Legal Title (Joint Tenants)
Pat	Pat	Saul	Equity
(TIC)	JT	JT	
$\left(\frac{2}{8}\right)$	$\frac{3}{8}$	$\frac{3}{8}$	

By definition, trustees of a trust for sale must sell. That notwithstanding, s25 LPA 1925 gives trustees a power to postpone sale provided that they act unanimously – in the absence of unanimity the duty to sell prevails: *Re Mayo* (4). Hence, Mike and Pat can agree to postpone sale. It would not avail Saul to rely on s26(3) LPA 1925 as that section only requires the trustees to consult the beneficiaries, and where practicable, give effect to the wishes of the majority. On the facts Pat has the majority interest ($^5/_8$), and anyway the trustees only have to consult not obey.

Saul could make an application to the court under s30 LPA 1925 for an order for sale, as he is clearly an interested party for the purposes of that section. In deciding whether or not to order sale the court will consider whether there was a secondary or collateral purpose to the trust, and whether that purpose still exists. If it does, sale will not be ordered: see *Jones* v *Challenger* (5); *Re Buchanan-Wollaston's Conveyance* (6). It could be argued that the secondary or collateral purpose lay in the fact that the purchase of the house was connected to the four's membership of the pop group and as the group has since disbanded, the secondary purpose has ceased to exist and sale should be ordered.

If sale is ordered pursuant to s30 LPA 1925 Saul will receive $^3/_8$ and Pat $^5/_8$ of the proceeds.

References

(1) [1986] AC 549
(2) (1861) 1 John & H 546
(3) [1975] Ch 429
(4) [1943] Ch 302
(5) [1961] 1 QB 176
(6) [1939] Ch 738

UNIVERSITY OF LONDON
LLB EXAMINATIONS 1993
for External Students
PART I EXAMINATION (Scheme A) and SECOND AND THIRD YEAR EXAMINATIONS (Scheme B)

LAND LAW

Tuesday, 8 June: 10.00 am to 1.00 pm

Answer *FOUR* of the following EIGHT questions

1 In 1980 John suggested to Mary, his mother, who was old and in poor health, that they should buy a house together. Mary agreed and, knowing that John had little money, offered to pay £50,000 towards the purchase price. The house, which was unregistered land, was conveyed into John's sole name. The purchase price of the house was £100,000 and the remaining £50,000 was raised by means of a building society mortgage for which John was solely responsible. Mary knew nothing of the mortgage. A few years later John obtained, again without Mary's knowledge, a loan of £70,000 from Quickloans Ltd, at a relatively high rate of interest, secured by a charge on the house in his sole name. Although Quickloans Ltd knew that Mary was living in the house, they made no inquiries of her. John used part of the £70,000 to redeem the first mortgage, pocketed the rest and disappeared. Quickloans subsequently sought possession of the house from Mary because the loan instalments have not been paid.

Advise Mary.

2 'No one by the light of nature ever understood an English mortgage of real estate.'

Outline the main criticisms that can be made of the English law of mortgages and suggest ways in which the law could be reformed to meet those criticisms.

3 Jim was the registered owner of Blackacre and in 1990 he orally agreed to sell a part of the land to his friend, Ben, for £20,000.

Ben did not pay anything, but he built a house on the part he had agreed to purchase and went into occupation. In 1922 Jim sold the whole of Blackacre to Victor and Victor was registered as the new owner. Victor has now told Ben to leave the land.

Advise Ben.

Would your advice be different if either (a) the agreement between Jim and Ben had been in writing, or (b) Blackacre had been sold to Victor expressly 'subject to Ben's rights'?

4 Consider the effect of

a) a lease of Redacre at a rent to Alf until he marries;

b) a lease of Pinkacre at a rent to Bill for five years which contains a covenant to renew on the same terms;

c) a lease of Greenacre at a yearly rent to Cal until the landlord requires the land for development, Cal goes into possession and pays rent yearly.

5 Jake owned a baker's shop and a yard behind the shop which served as a carpark for his customers. Jake also owned the track that led from the highway along the side of the shop to the yard. On the other side of the track was Sid's carpentry shop and in 1965 Jake executed a deed granting Sid a 'licence' to use the track and to park his van in the carpark. This made it possible for Sid to deliver timber to the back of his shop and he therefore built a rear extension to the shop for the purpose of storing the timber. In 1991 Sid sold his shop to William, who has since expanded the carpentry business. Not only does William park his van in Jake's carpark, but William's two young apprentices also park their motorcycles there. Jake has now written to William demanding that he cease to use the track and the carpark and informing William of his intention to convert the carpark into a cafe for his customers.

Advise William.

6 When Stella decided to buy a farm, she invited her lover, Paul, to come and live with her and help her run the farm. Stella paid the whole purchase price and the farm was conveyed into her sole name. When Paul asked why it had not been conveyed into their joint names, Stella told him that there was no need for him to worry as he would get a half-share when they got married and as she was going to leave him her London apartment in her will anyway. Stella and Paul never married but they worked hard on the farm for several years, sharing the profits equally, and as a result the value of the farm doubled. Recently Stella has

died leaving all her estate to her mother. Paul now claims both the farm and the London apartment.

Advise Stella's mother.

7 In 1989 Leslie granted Alice a lease of Redstone House (unregistered land) for 20 years, Alice covenanting, *inter alia,* to pay a yearly rent of £10,000, to keep the house in a good state of repair and not to use the house for immoral purposes. In 1990 Alice assigned her lease to Bert and in 1993 Bert granted a sublease to Chris for five years. In 1993 Leslie assigned his reversion to Rachel. No rent has been paid since 1991, the house is in serious need of repair and Chris has recently been convicted to keeping a brothel.

Who has remedies against whom in respect of these breaches of covenant?

8 'The 1925 legislation has endowed trusts for sale with all the advantages of settled land. Little would be lost if all settlements were made to take effect as trusts for sale.'

Discuss.

QUESTION 1

General Comment

A fairly standard question on the acquisition and protection of an equitable interest in land, except that a good understanding and application of the principles relating to a party's implied consent to a mortgage is essential to a good answer.

Skeleton Solution

Resulting trust.

Overreaching.

Notice.

Caunce v *Caunce.*

Kingsnorth Finance v *Tizard.*

Implied consent.

Paddington Building Society v *Mendelsohn.*

Equity & Law Home Loans v *Prestidge.*

Suggested Solution

The first issue is whether Mary has an interest in the house. As the house is conveyed into John's sole name, it is clear that Mary does not have a legal interest in it, therefore any interest she has must be equitable. There is no suggestion that the conveyance spells out any trust in favour of Mary, so she cannot rely on *Goodman* v *Gallant* (1).

However, Mary has contributed £50,000 towards the purchase of the house costing £100,000, and as there is nothing to indicate that she intended this as a gift or loan, she will acquire a beneficial interest in the house under a resulting trust. Consequently, there is a co-ownership situation which finds expression in an implied or statutory trust for sale (ss34-36 Law of Property Act (LPA) 1925). John holds the house on trust for sale for himself and Mary in proportion to their respective contributions.

As the house stands in an area of land governed by the Land Charges Act 1925, Mary cannot protect her beneficial interest by registering a land charge (classes A-F). As her interest arises behind a trust it is a non-registrable but overreachable one. That being so, Quickloans could take free of it if they have overreached it according to s2 Law of Property Act 1925. However, it appears that Quickloans only ever dealt with John (the sole legal owner), and as such, they have not dealt with or paid two trustees and have not overreached.

Despite the fact that Quickloans have not overreached, they will only be bound by Mary's interest if it can be shown that they had notice of it and that Mary did not impliedly consent to the mortgage.

As far as notice goes, a non-registrable but overreachable interest which has not been overreached, is binding on everyone except the purchaser without notice – actual, constructive or imputed. Quickloans does not have personal knowledge of Mary's interest and thus does not have actual notice. They may, however, have constructive or imputed notice. Constructive notice exists where the purchaser would have discovered the existence of the equitable interest if he had investigated properly or at all. Imputed notice is simply constructive notice of an agent.

According to *Caunce* v *Caunce* (2), a purchaser of property vested in the sole legal title of a husband does not have notice of a wife's equitable interest by virtue of her actual occupation. In such cases the wife's presence is said to be wholly consistent with the sole legal title offered by the husband. By analogy it could be said that even if Quickloans were aware of Mary's presence in the house that could be explained on the basis that she was there simply because she was John's mother – in other words that her presence was wholly consistent with the sole legal title offered by John. On this basis Quickloans would take free of Mary's interest.

On the other hand, according to *Kingsnorth Finance* v *Tizard* (3), where a purchaser is aware that some other person is in occupation of the premises he should undertake further investigations to see whether that person has an interest. Failure to do so will mean that the purchaser is subject to all equitable interests he would have discovered if he had investigated properly or at all. On the facts, as Quickloans knew that Mary was living in the house they should have made further enquiries to see whether she had an interest. Their failure to do so would mean that they were subject to her interest unless it can be shown that Mary impliedly consented to the mortgage.

When the house was first purchased, Mary was well aware that John had little money, but it is not clear whether she knew what the value of the house was. If she did, it could be argued that she must have realised that a mortgage was necessary in order to purchase the house, and, therefore could be said to have impliedly consented to the building society mortgage (see *Paddington Building Society* v *Mendelsohn* (4)). If that is the case, then when John took the mortgage from Quickloans and used it to pay off the first building society, Mary's implied consent to the amount of the first mortgage is deemed to be an implied consent to that amount of the Quickloans mortgage (*Equity & Law Home Loans Ltd* v *Prestidge* (5)).

Therefore, should Quickloans succeed in obtaining possession of the property and selling it, unless Prestidge applies in their favour, Mary would have an interest which takes priority over theirs and which must be defrayed out of the expenses of sale before the mortgage monies are recovered.

References

(1) [1986] Fam 106
(2) [1969] 1 WLR 286
(3) [1986] 1 WLR 783
(4) (1985) 50 P & CR 244
(5) [1992] 1 WLR 137

QUESTION 2

General Comment

Not a write all you know about mortgages question! The question demands a critique of the law of mortgages, and therefore a knowledge of the Law Commission's proposals is essential to a good answer.

Skeleton Solution

Definition.

Methods of creation.

Priorities.

Postponing redemption.

Collateral advantages.

Consumer Credit Act 1974.

Suggested Solution

A mortgage is simply security for a loan redeemable upon repayment of the loan. However, unlike the definition, the realities and practicalities of mortgages are very complex, and as Lord MacNaghten noted in *Samuel* v *Jarrah Timber and Wood Paving Corporation Ltd* (1) 'No one ever understood an English mortgage of real estate'.

Criticisms of the English mortgage can be made across the board form creation to priorities, including mortgagees' rights. Although the method of creating mortgages has simplified since the 1925 property legislation, the whole process is still cumbersome. Legal mortgages no longer involve a conveyance of the fee simple but instead are created by a demise for a term of years absolute or by legal charge – the latter being simpler and the preferred option. However, English law does recognise the creation of equitable mortgages which, under the Law of Property (Miscellaneous Provisions) Act 1989, must be created by a written contract containing all of the relevant terms and signed by both parties. It is readily apparent, that the law of mortgages suffers from the same defects which were apparent in land law prior to the

1925 legislation, namely a plethora of interests both legal and equitable which can exist in the same piece of land. To remedy this the Law Commission recommended in its report on Land Mortgages No 99, that all the existing methods of creating mortgages be abolished and replaced by a Formal Land Mortgage created by statute.

The logical consequence of the recognition of legal and equitable mortgages is the operation of two different schemes of protection and complex rules for determining priorities of mortgages. Legal mortgagees either protect themselves by taking title deeds, registering legal charges or puisne mortgagees (Ci land charge), whereas equitable mortgagees have to register general equitable charges (Ciii). Where registration is required for protection, the normal rules apply making a mortgage void against a subsequent purchaser for want of registration. The adoption of a single form of statutory mortgage would render the differing forms and methods of protection unnecessary.

Because of the different types of mortgage, complex rules have evolved governing the determination of priorities between competing mortgages. Generally speaking, legal mortgages prevail over equitable, and the first in time has priority. However, a prior mortgagee who has taken the title deeds for protection can lose that priority through fraud estoppel or gross negligence (*Hewitt* v *Loosemore* (2); *Agra Bank* v *Barry* (3)). As far as equitable mortgages are concerned they are governed by the rule in *Dearle* v *Hall* (4) (as amended by s138 and s139 Law of Property Act 1925), which provides that priority deeds in the order in which notice of the mortgage is received by the owner of the legal estate. Again the adoption of a single statutory mortgage which must be registered would eradicate this problem.

Although the law will not allow a mortgage which is irredeemable (*Fairclough* v *Swan Brewery Co Ltd* (5)), a term in a mortgage which postpones redemption until the end of the mortgage can be valid if it is not oppressive or unconscionable (*Knightsbridge Estates Trust Ltd* v *Byrne* (6)). This means that the mortgagor is prevented from redeeming until the end of the mortgage and must continue to pay interest on the loan for the whole of that period. In the meantime his dealing with the land will always be against the backdrop of the mortgage and subject to, (in most cases), the mortgagee's legal charge – a situation which makes it difficult to use the land as collateral and which does not promote alienability of the land, one of the reasons for the 1925 legislation. Mortgages governed by the Consumer Credit Act 1974 are prohibited from containing such a term by s94 of the Act which gives the debtor (mortgagor) a statutory right of early redemption. The Law Commission considered that a similar provision could be adopted for all mortgages, which would effectively render postponement impossible.

Other problems arise in the context of collateral advantages – terms in a mortgage which are designed to give the mortgagee something more than his security and interest. The relevant principles can be stated as follows: a collateral advantage which exists until redemption can be valid, but will be void if it is oppressive or unconscionable; a collateral advantage which exists beyond redemption is void unless it exists as an independent transaction (see eg *Noakes* v *Rice* (7); *Biggs* v *Hodinott* (8)). Where valid, the existence of a collateral advantage has two major consequences. Firstly, the mortgagor may find that he is 'tied-in' to the mortgagee in a business sense (for example, that during the course of the mortgage he has to buy all his stock from the mortgagee), a situation which could actually last for the whole of the mortgage if the right to redeem has been effectively postponed. Secondly, the mortgage then becomes a valuable asset for the mortgagee, even more so if the right to redeem has been postponed. These problems could be eradicated, to a greater or lesser extent, by the enactment of a statute similar to the Consumer Credit Act which prohibits any term designed to recover more than security and interest, and/or by making the mortgagee's assignment of the mortgage dependent on the consent of the mortgagor.

Additionally, criticism may be levelled at rates of interest imposed in mortgages. Obviously, if an exceptionally high rate of interest is imposed or is disguised as a collateral advantage, then if it is found to be oppressive and unconscionable it will be struck down (*Cityland and Property (Holdings) Ltd* v *Dabrah* (9)). In the case of Consumer Credit Act mortgages, if the rate of interest is found to be extortinate the court has the power to re-open and re-write the agreement. Although a similar statutory power would (arguably), be more appropriate than the existing common law approach, it must be borne in mind that as currently drafted the Consumer Credit Act does recognise a creditor's right to charge high rates of interest (see *Ketley* v *Scott* (10) – 48% APR was valid).

As far as the mortgagee's remedies go, the main criticism lies in the existence of the right to foreclose. The courts have shown themselves extremely reluctant to allow a mortgagee to foreclose, preferring instead to order sale (which at least means that any excess capital monies after paying off expenses and mortgage go to the mortgagor). In the circumstances the time may well have come for this remedy to be abolished – again a matter considered by the Law Commission.

Similarly, when a mortgagee goes into possession either as a prelude to sale or as a means of recovering interest, with the exception of the principle of wilful default, the mortgagor has no effective means of controlling the mortgagee or of making him account for any benefit he receives. As before the adoption of a statutory requirement of accountability would go some way to cure this defect.

Given the criticisms that could be levelled at the law of mortgages, essential reforms would appear to be required in respect of creation and registration of mortgages as well as the content of the agreement. This would probably best be achieved by the enactment of a single act drawing upon some of the principles enshrined in the Consumer Credit Act 1974.

References

(1) [1904] AC 323
(2) (1851) 9 Hare 449
(3) (1874) LR 7 HL 135
(4) (1828) 3 Russ 1
(5) [1912] AC 565
(6) [1939] Ch 441
(7) [1902] AC 24
(8) [1898] 2 Ch 307
(9) [1968] Ch 116
(10) [1981] ICR 241

QUESTION 3

General Comment

Formalities for a contract of sale are at the heart of this question. It is therefore necessary to deal with s2 Law of Property (Miscellaneous Provisions) Act 1989. Thereafter this is a straightforward question on estoppel, registration and notice.

Skeleton Solution

Law of Property (Miscellaneous Provisions) Act 1989.
Estoppel.
Section 70(1)(g) Land Registration Act 1925.
Lyus v *Prowsa*.
Peffer v *Rigg*.
Binions v *Evans*.

Suggested Solution

In order for there to be a valid contract of sale in respect of Blackacre there must be compliance with s2 Law of Property (Miscellaneous Provisions) Act 1989. That Act requires the contract to be in writing, contain all the relevant terms and be signed by both parties. If not the contract is void. As the contract between Jim and Ben is oral only, it is void and no action can be brought on it. It follows that as the contract is void it cannot form the basis of an estate contract and be registered as a minor interest under the Land Registration Act 1925.

Nonetheless Ben has, with the knowledge of Jim, gone onto the land and built a house on it. As Jim has, apparently, stood back and allowed or tacitly encouraged Ben to spend money on his (Jim's) land, it could be argued that a proprietary estoppel arises in Ben's favour (see *Willmott* v *Barber* (1); *Taylor Fashions* v *Liverpool Victoria Trustees* (2)). If an estoppel arises in favour of Ben being of a proprietary nature, he could have protected it against subsequent purchasers by entering on a minor interest (in the form of a notice, caution or restriction). There is nothing to say that Ben has done so and consequently it would be void against Victor as a subsequent purchaser (s20, s59(6) Land Registration Act 1925).

However, Ben may be able to argue that he has an overriding interest in the land under s70(1)(g) Land Registration Act 1925. He is in occupation of the land prior to the sale to Victor and he has a proprietary interest in the land by virtue of the estoppel. Therefore, provided Victor has not asked Ben whether he has an interest which he (Ben) deliberately concealed, all the elements of s70(1)(g) would appear to be present. In these circumstances Victor would be bound by the interest unless he took the conveyance from, and paid the capital monies to two trustees (s2 Law of Property Act 1925 – *Williams and Glyn's Bank* v *Boland* (3), *City of London Building Society* v *Flegg* (4)).

a) *If the agreement were in writing*
If the agreement were in writing it would comply with s2 Law of Property (Miscellaneous Provisions) Act 1989, and form the basis of a registrable estate contract. It could be protected by entering on a minor interest. Failure to do so would, as discussed above, make it void against Victor, but Ben may be able to rely on s70(1)(g).

b) *'Subject to Ben's rights'*
If the land had been sold expressly subject to Ben's rights, due to his knowledge Victor may be held to be a constructive trustee of the land for Ben even if Ben has not entered on a minor interest (see *Lyus* v *Prowsa Developments Ltd* (5); *Peffer* v *Rigg* (6); and *Binions* v *Evans* (7)). This outcome has been the subject of much criticism especially as it runs counter to the clear wording of s20 and s59(6) Land Registration Act 1925.

References

(1) (1880) 15 Ch D 96
(2) [1982] QB 133
(3) [1981] AC 487
(4) [1988] AC 54
(5) [1982] 1 WLR 1044
(6) [1977] 1 WLR 285
(7) [1972] Ch 359

QUESTION 4

General Comment

A variation on the usual kind of question dealing with types of leases. The question centres on the relationship between s149(6) Law of Property Act 1925, s145 Law of Property Act 1922 and certainty of duration.

Skeleton Solution

Characterisation of a lease.

Section 149(6) Law of Property Act 1925.

Section 145 Law of Property Act 1922.

Parkus v *Greenwood*.

Marjorie Burnett v *Barclay*.

Certainty of duration.

Periodic leases.

Lace v *Chantler*.

Prudential Assurance Co Ltd v *London Residuary Body*.

Suggested Solution

For a valid lease or tenancy to exist four things must be satisfied. Firstly, the premises must be sufficiently defined; secondly, exclusive possession must have been granted; thirdly, the term or duration must be certain; and fourthly, leases in excess of three years must be granted by deed, whereas periodic tenancies can come into existence without the need for writing at all. Periodic tenancies come into existence through the acts of taking possession and paying rent – the period of the tenancy being determined by the period over which rent is calculated.

a) By virtue of s149(6) Law of Property Act 1925, leases at a rent for life or lives or until the marriage of the lessee (as in Albert's case) are converted into leases for a term of 90 years. Albert therefore has a lease for 90 years which can be determined after his marriage by either party giving one month's written notice to expire on one of the quarter days.

b) A lease for five years with a covenant to renew on the same terms could be a perpetually renewable lease under s145 Law of Property Act 1922. It is a question of construction whether there is a perpetually renewable lease, with the courts tending to lean against such a finding. Basically, if the covenant for renewal is part of a separate obligation then there is no perpetually renewable lease (see *Marjorie Burnett* v *Barclay* (1)), but if the lease is to be renewed on the existing terms 'including the covenant for renewal', then there will be a perpetually renewable lease (*Parkus* v *Greenwood* (2)).

If, on construction, Bill is found to have a perpetually renewable lease, then under s145 of the Act it will be converted into a term of 2,000 years, which can only be determined by the tenant by giving 10 days' notice to expire on the date on which, but for the operation of the statute, the lease would have determined. In other words by Bill giving 10 days' notice to expire at the end of the five year term.

Moreover, if it is found to be perpetually renewable, Bill could, of course assign it provided the assignment is registered with the landlord within six months of it taking place. However, unlike other leases, upon assignment the assignee (Bill) ceases to be liable even in contract for breaches committed after the assignment by the assignor.

c) The problem for Cal here is to establish that there is certainty of duration. In order for a lease for a fixed term to be valid it must have a certain duration (see *Lace* v *Chantler* (3) – where a lease for the duration of the war was void). This principle was reaffirmed in *Prudential Assurance Co Ltd* v *London Residuary Body* (4), where the House of Lords said that the principle in *Lace* applied to all leases and tenancy agreements, and that a lease 'until the land was required for widening the road' was void because the period was uncertain. Therefore, following *Prudential* Cal could not claim to have a lease for a fixed term, as a lease 'until the land is required for development' is equally uncertain.

However, Cal has gone into possession and pays rent yearly, the combined effect of which is to establish a periodic tenancy in his favour – the period being determined by reference to which the rent is calculated. In Cal's case the rent is assessed yearly and hence there would appear to be a yearly periodic tenancy. Generally speaking yearly leases can be determined by such notice as the parties agree, failing which a half year's notice to expire on one of the normal quarter days is required.

Unfortunately for Cal, the House of Lords also held in *Prudential* that a grant for an uncertain term which takes the form of a yearly tenancy which cannot be determined by the landlord, does not create a lease. In that case although the plaintiffs had gone into possession paying a yearly rent, there could only be a yearly tenancy if the terms of the agreement were such that both the landlord and tenant could give half a year's notice, and that the term preventing the landlord giving notice until the land was required for road widening was inconsistent with a yearly tenancy. On the facts Cal would be in the same position, and his lease would be determinable upon six months' notice.

References

(1) (1980) 258 EG 642
(2) [1950] Ch 644
(3) [1944] KB 368
(4) [1992] 3 WLR 279

QUESTION 5

General Comment

A question which requires the candidate to distinguish between easements and licences. The principles relating to the acquisition of leases are important. Candidates should not try to put square pegs into round holes – (if it is not an easement do not try to make it one).

Skeleton Solution

Re Ellenborough.

Accommodation.

Exclusive possession.

Newman v *Jones.*

London & Blenheim Estates Ltd v *Ladbroke Retail Parks Ltd.*

Acquisition.

Express grant.

Section 62 Law of Property Act 1925.

Licences.

Estoppel.

Ashburn v *Arnold.*

Suggested Solution

An easement is a right in or over the land of another. In order to be an easement the right in question must satisfy the characteristics in *Re Ellenborough Park* (1), and must be properly acquired as an easement.

In this case William's continued use of the track and car park will depend on whether he can establish an easement in his favour. In the first place *Re Ellenborough* must be satisfied.

On the facts Jake's land would be the servient land and William's land the dominant, hence the first requirement of *Ellenborough* is satisfied. Secondly, the right of way and of parking must accommodate William's land. In other words, the rights must be more than personal – they must be of a proprietary nature (see

Hill v *Tupper* (2), contra *Moody* v *Steggles* (3)). In so far as the rights in question are connected to the running of the business from the dominant land they may be said to be proprietary. Equally, they could be said to make the dominant land a better or more convenient property and to increase its value, factors which were recognised in *Ellenborough* itself as amounting to accommodation of the dominant land. Thirdly, as both pieces of land are not owned and occupied by the same person the third element of *Ellenborough* is satisfied.

Finally, the rights claimed must be capable of forming the subject matter of grant – they could have been granted by deed. There appears to have been a capable grantor (Jake) and grantee (Sid), rights of way and parking are recognised as being sufficiently definite to be easements and, finally, the right to use the track (which is essentially a right of way) is undoubtedly in the nature of recognised easements. As far as the parking goes, easements to park have been recognised (see *Newman* v *Jones* (4); *London & Blenheim Estates Ltd* v *Ladbroke Retail Parks Ltd* (5)) despite the fact that the law is generally wary about recognising as easements rights which amount to a claim to exclusive or joint possession of all or part of the servient land (see *Copeland* v *Greenhalf* (6)).

Subject to the exclusive possession point, it appears that both the rights in question have the characteristics of an easement.

In terms of acquisition, although Jake granted Sid a licence, he did not expressly grant him an easement (*IDC Group Ltd* v *Clark* (7)). Neither is there any evidence of the need to imply an easement of necessity or common intention. Section 62 Law of Property Act is not applicable as there has never, according to the facts, been a conveyance by Jake to Sid, and therefore Sid has nothing which he can pass on to William (*Quicke* v *Chapman* (8)). Similarly, *Wheeldon* v *Burrows* (9) is inapplicable as there is nothing to suggest that Jake ever owned both dominant and servient land. Prescription cannot apply, not least because there is not a long enough period of user and the use has been with permission.

In the circumstances, whilst the rights in question have the characteristics of an easement, they do not appear to have been acquired as such.

It would appear then that what Sid had was a licence to use the track and car park. It could be that Sid had merely a bare licence, and in so far as Jake allowed William the same right of access he too had the same. If so, the licence would be revocable at any time and William and employees would become trespassers upon expiry of a reasonable time. Alternatively, it could be argued that there was a contractual licence with the deed forming the consideration. If this was the case, the better view is that such licences are personal only and would only operate in favour of the contracting parties (Jake and Sid), so that William would acquire no rights under it (see *King* v *David Allen Billposting* (10); *Clore* v *Theatrical Properties Limited* (11); and *Ashburn Anstalt* v *Arnold* (12)).

Alternatively, Sid may be able to argue that he has an estoppel licence by virtue of the fact that he has extended his shop in order to store timber and Jake stood by and tacitly allowed or encouraged him to do so. In other words, if Sid can show that Jake's conduct was such as to make it inequitable for him to deny the existence of the right to use the path and to park (*Taylor Fashions* v *Liverpool Victoria Trustees* (13)). If the estoppel arises then it can operate in favour of William, who may be able to use the same argument himself given that he has expanded the business. The court would, of course, have to decide how best to satisfy any estoppel which may mean that William will be entitled to continue to use the path and park.

References

(1) [1951] Ch 131
(2) (1863) 2 H & C 121
(3) (1879) 12 Ch D 261
(4) (1982) March unreported
(5) [1993] 1 All ER 307
(6) [1952] Ch 488
(7) (1992) The Times 23 July
(8) [1903] 1 Ch 655
(9) (1879) 12 Ch D 31
(10) [1916] 2 AC 54
(11) [1936] 3 All ER 483
(12) [1985] Ch 1
(13) [1982] QB 133

QUESTION 6

General Comment

A standard question on the acquisition of interests in land dealing with resulting trusts, constructive trusts and proprietary estoppel. A knowledge of the decision in *Hammond* v *Mitchell* would be useful.

Skeleton Solution

Conveyance.

Goodman v *Gallant*.

Resulting trust.

Gissing v *Gissing*.

Constructive trust.

Informal agreement.

Lloyds Bank v *Rosset*.

Eves v *Eves*.

Detriment.

Hammond v *Mitchell*.

Estoppel.

Re Basham.

Grant v *Edwards*.

Suggested Solution

The main issue here is whether Paul has any interest in the farm or London apartment.

As both the farm and apartment were vested in Stella's sole name, clearly Paul has no legal interest in them. Furthermore, there is no evidence to suggest that conveyances contained a trust in favour of Paul (contra: *Goodman* v *Gallant* (1)). In the circumstances, if Paul is to have an interest he must have acquired it by way of resulting or constructive trust or by way of proprietary estoppel.

Farm

As regards the farm, Stella paid the whole of the purchase price thus ruling out any form of direct financial contribution by Paul to its acquisition. Furthermore, there is no evidence of Paul making any form of indirect contribution which would entitle him to an interest under a resulting trust (*Pettitt* v *Pettitt* (2); *Gissing* v *Gissing* (3)).

In order to claim an interest under a constructive trust Paul would have to argue that there was either an express informal agreement between the parties which he acted upon to his detriment, or that an agreement should be imputed between them giving him an interest (see Lord Bridge in *Lloyds Bank* v *Rosset* (4)).

As for the former, it might be argued that Stella's excuse for not putting the farm into joint names was evidence of an agreement between the parties that he should have an interest, in much the same way as in *Eves* v *Eves* (5), *Cooke* v *Head* (6) and *Grant* v *Edwards* (7). It does not matter that such an agreement came into existence after the acquisition of the farm, for as Lord Bridge stated in *Rossett*, in exceptional cases the agreement could come into existence at a later date. In any event Paul would have to produce cogent evidence of the agreement. If Paul can establish the existence of the agreement he also needs to show that he has acted to his detriment in reliance upon it. Clearly, Paul participated fully in the farm business and it may be argued that his involvement in the commercial venture was enough to give him an interest in the land (see *Hammond* v *Mitchell* (8)). Alternatively, it could be said that there was no agreement that he should have an interest and the share of the profits was his only reward.

As regards the latter, the court would analyse the subsequent conduct of the parties to see whether they are sufficient to spell out some presumed intention on the part of the parties. Clearly, Paul's hard work would indicate that he should have some share, but, it could be argued, that should be limited to a share in the profits only. If a constructive trust arises in favour of Paul, his actual occupation coupled with the interest under the trust would give him an overriding interest in land under s70(1)(g) Land Registration Act 1925, which would be binding on Stella's mother (*Williams & Glyn's Bank* v *Boland* (9)).

If Paul's claim to an interest under a constructive trust were to fail, he could rely on estoppel as in *Grant* v *Edwards* (7). In order to do so, he would have to show the existence of a representation and reliance as in the case of a constructive trust (indeed in *Lloyds Bank* v *Rosset* they were recognised as being very similar doctrines). As described above, Stella's statement to Paul could be seen as the representation. As in the case of the constructive trust, Paul's wholehearted participation in the commercial activities on the farm could be seen as a detriment and evidence that he had acted consistently with the representation (*Hammond*).

If an estoppel arises in favour of Paul, the task for the court will be how best to satisfy it, and the court will do the minimum necessary to do justice to the estopel (*Crabb* v *Arun District Council* (10)). The precise remedy appears largely to depend on the representation in that the applicant gets what he has been promised, be that the transfer of fee simple (*Pascoe* v *Turner* (11)) or a life interest (*Inwards* v *Baker* (12)). On this basis, if the representation is that Paul will get a one share that is what the court will award.

Apartment

The same principles as discussed above in relation to the farm are relevant when considering the claims to the apartment. As in the case of the farm, Paul has made no direct financial contributions which would justify an interest by way of resulting trust.

Furthermore, such acts as he has done to his detriment appear to relate exclusively to the acquisition of an interest in the farm and not the apartment. Those activities were not of a nature which would justify the inference of an intended proprietary interest in his favour in the apartment (see *Hammond*).

As far as proprietary estoppel is concerned, whilst it is possible for a promise of a future interest to found an estoppel (see *Re Basham* (13)), the problem for Paul here is largely the same as that connected with constructive trusts, viz, his acts are acts of detriment connected to the farm not the apartment (*Hammond*).

In the circumstances, it appears that Paul will have a better prospect of claiming an interest in the farm, be it by constructive trust or proprietary estoppel, than he will in the apartment.

References

(1) [1986] Fam 106
(2) [1970] AC 777
(3) [1971] AC 886
(4) [1990] 1 All ER 1111
(5) [1975] 1 WLR 1338
(6) [1972] 1 WLR 518
(7) [1986] Ch 638
(8) [1992] 2 All ER 109
(9) [1981] AC 487
(10) [1976] Ch 179
(11) [1979] 1 WLR 431
(12) [1965] 2 QB 29
(13) [1986] 1 WLR 1498

QUESTION 7

General Comment

A typical question on leasehold covenants. The question requires an exposition of the rules relating to the transmissibility of leasehold covenants and not an answer devoted wholly, or mainly, to remedies.

Skeleton Solution

Privity of estate.
Privity of contract.
Spencer's Case.
Tulk v *Moxhay.*
Sections 141 and 142 Law of Property Act 1925.
Forfeiture.
Section 146 Law of Property Act 1925.
Landlord and Tenant Act 1927.
Distress.
Arrears.

Suggested Solution

Leslie and Alice
In 1989 when Leslie granted Alice a lease for 20 years, there existed between the parties a contract (the lease being simply a form of contract) and privity of estate (a relationship of landlord and tenant with Leslie being the landlord). Between Leslie and Alice the covenants in the lease, whether expressed (repairs and user) or implied (payment of rent), are enforceable in contract, and their contractual liability is a continuing one lasting for the whole period of the lease even though in the interim they may have assigned their interests (*Celsteel* v *Alton House Holdings* (1)).

Alice assigns to Bert
In 1990 Alice assigned her lease to Bert, thereby ceasing to be tenant and destroying privity of estate with Leslie. Alice does, of course, remain liable to Leslie in contract. The effect of the

assignment is that Bert steps into Alice's shoes provided the principles in *Spencer's Case* (2) are satisfied. Firstly, the assignment must be by deed, and, secondly, there must be a complete assignment of the whole term. If these are satisfied then the benefit and burden of all covenants touching and concerning the land run to the assignee (Bert). Covenants which affect the landlord as landlord and the tenant as tenant touch and concern the land; personal covenants do not. In the present case all three covenants could touch and concern the land, so that under *Spencer's Case* the benefit and burden of them will run to Bert. At this stage there exists privity of estate between Leslie and Bert (a relationship of landlord and tenant) but not privity of contract.

Bert sub-leases to Chris

A sub-lease differs from an assignment in that the sub-lessor (Bert) retains a reversionary interest in the lease. Therefore at this stage, Leslie is the landlord, Bert is the tenant and Chris the sub-tenant. As between Leslie and Chris there exists neither privity of contract nor estate. The burden of the covenants cannot have run to Chris as there has been no assignment and he will only be bound by them if they have run under the doctrine in *Tulk* v *Moxhay* (3) which requires the covenants to be negative in nature (*Haywood* v *Brunswick Permanent Benefit Building Society* (4) – of the three covenants only the user covenant is negative in nature).

As between Bert and Chris there exists both privity of contract and estate – Bert is Chris's immediate landlord. Therefore, if Bert had inserted the same covenants in his lease with Chris as exist in the head lease, Chris will be bound by them.

As mentioned above, between Leslie and Bert there already exists privity of estate.

Leslie assigns reversion to Rachel

For there to be a valid assignment of the reversion it must be by deed, and provided this is satisfied s141 and s142 Law of Property Act 1925 have the effect of passing to the assignee the benefit of burden of all covenants which have reference to the subject matter of the lease (which is little more than a statutory formulation of touch and concern the land). Consequently, Rachel steps into the shoes of Leslie and can sue in respect of breaches committed prior to the assignment of the reversion provided they have not been expressly or impliedly waived by Leslie.

By 1993, Rachel is the landlord, Bert the tenant and Chris the sub-tenant. There exists between Rachel and Bert privity of estate just as existed between Leslie and Bert; between Rachel and Chris neither privity of estate nor contract, and between Bert and Chris privity of estate and contract.

Clearly the covenants have been breached, and according to the basic provisions of enforceability, Rachel can commence an action against anyone with whom she had privity of estate even for breaches committed prior to the assignment of the reversion to her.

Rachel v Bert

Accordingly, Rachel's primary cause of action will lie against Bert (subject to any waiver). In respect of the breach of the rent covenant she has several possible remedies, namely, an action for arrears, distress or an action for possession. There is no need for her to issue a formal demand under the Common Law Procedure Act 1852 as the arrears exceed six months.

Provided there is a forfeiture clause, Rachel could forfeit the lease against Bert. To do so for breach of the user clause she would have to issue a notice under s146 Law of Property Act 1925. As the premises would be tainted with immorality (*Rugby School* v *Tannahill* (5)) the breach would not be capable of remedy and it is extremely unlikely that relief from forfeiture would be granted.

As for the breach of the repairing covenant, Rachel's initial remedy against Bert would be a claim for damages under the Landlord and Tenant Act 1927 – the measure being the fall in the value of the reversion. Failing that, she could forfeit the lease (if there was a forfeiture clause) by issuing a s146 notice suitably amended to inform Bert of his rights under the Leasehold Property Repairs Act 1938.

In any of the cases, if Rachel applies for forfeiture, Bert could apply for relief from forfeiture, as could Chris as sub-tenant. If relief is refused Chris's sub-lease, being a lesser interest, would fold with Bert's lease.

Bert v Chris

As Rachel's primary cause of action is against Bert, he in turn may have certain rights against Chris. Firstly, Bert may be able to rely on an implied indemnity whereby Chris indemnifies him for any breaches committed by him (Chris). Secondly, Bert may be able to rely on an express indemnity if he has inserted such a clause in his lease with Chris (s77 Law of Property Act 1925).

Rachel v Chris

Although Rachel cannot sue Chris directly due to lack of privity, she will be able to obtain an injunction (mandatory) to prevent the premises being used as a brothel because the burden of the user covenant will have run with the land to Chris under the doctrine in *Tulk* v *Moxhay*. For this to happen the covenant must be negative in substance (which this clearly is), and there must be an intention that the burden should run (s79 Law of Property Act 1925).

Leslie v Alice

As mentioned above, Alice remains liable to Leslie in contract throughout the term of the lease. Consequently, she could be sued on this basis, but may well be able to rely on an express or implied indemnity.

References

(1) [1986] 1 WLR 666
(2) (1583) 5 Co Rep 16
(3) (1848) 2 Ph 774
(4) (1881) 8 QBD 403
(5) [1934] 1 KB 695

QUESTION 8

General Comment

This is not a write everything you know about settlements and trusts for sale, or a general comparison between the two. What is required is an analysis of the position of the tenant for life and trustees of the settlement with that of the trustees for sale.

Skeleton Solution

Settled Land Act 1925.

Law of Property Act 1925.

Section 19 Settled Land Act.

Tenant for life's powers.

Wheelwright v *Walker*.

Limitation.

Section 106 Settled Land Act.

Re Trenchard.

Re Orlebar.

Role of trustees of settlement.

Powers of trustees for sale.

Section 28 Law of Property Act 1925.

Section 25 Law of Property Act.

Re Inns

Suggested Solution

The 1925 property legislation recognised two ways of settling land which have certain similarities but which, arguably, were intended to achieve different things. Traditional thinking has it that strict settlements (governed by the Settled Land Act 1925), are designed to keep property in the family whereas trusts for sale (governed by the Law of Property Act 1925), are to be used as a vehicle to ensure easier alienability of land.

The essence of the strict settlement is that the tenant for life – a beneficiary of full age and immediately entitled to possession of the land – holds the legal title to the property as well as his own beneficial interest. The tenant for life has a number of powers in respect of the legal estate. For instance, he can sell the settled estate although as a fiduciary for the remaindermen he must get the best price reasonably obtainable (*Wheelwright* v *Walker* (1)). He can also exchange or lease the land, and, as in the case of sale, he is under an obligation to get the best rent reasonably obtainable. Additionally, the tenant for life can grant options over the land and mortgage or charge it for limited purposes, the golden rule being that the land can only be mortgaged for the benefit of the settled land.

As well as these powers the tenant for life has a host of minor powers, eg to cut and sell timber, to sell the principal mansion house and to compromise claims. The Act provides that the powers of the tenant for life cannot be curtailed in any way (s106 Settled Land Act 1925), so that any term in the settlement which is designed to prevent him from exercising his powers is void (*Re Trenchard* (2); *Re Orlebar* (3)), with the result that the tenant for life could validly sell the land thus defeating the supposed object of keeping it in the family. The corollary of s106 is s104 which provides that a tenant for life cannot assign, release or contract not to exercise his powers.

As for the role of the trustees of the settlement, that is peripheral. Their main task is to receive and hold capital monies following overreaching and to invest it at the direction of the tenant for life. In addition they are to receive notification from the tenant for life that he intends to exercise his powers and give consent where appropriate.

Although the trust for sale was, theoretically, designed to operate in a different way to the settlement, in fact it can achieve all that the settlement can. For a start, the trustees for sale, who may also be the beneficiaries, are given all the powers of a tenant for life and the trustees of the settlement under s28 Law of Property Act (LPA) 1925.

Moreover, in some respects much would be achieved by converting settlements into trusts. The trust for sale has several advantages over the settlement; for instance, it is simpler to create – it is not necessary to have two documents as in the case of a settlement and ss34-36 LPA 1925 brings trusts for sale into existence automatically in cases of co-ownership. Secondly, unlike the tenant for life, the trustees can delegate their powers to a person of full age who is beneficially entitled (s29 LPA 1925). Thirdly, and paradoxically, the trust for sale is a much better device for keeping land in the family if that is what is desired. It can be achieved either by the trustees exercising their power to postpone sale (s25 LPA

1925), or by making sale dependent on the consent of a named person (*Re Inns* (4)). Fourthly, strict settlements only apply to realty, whereas trusts for sale can be used for both personalty and realty. Consequently, the settlor can deal with both in the one trust whereas if he wishes to create a strict settlement that must be done under a separate trust from the trust of personalty. Fifthly, Trusts for Sale are a much better way of giving concurrent interest to beneficiaries.

Clearly, there are undoubted benefits in replacing settlements with trusts for sale as the Law Commission recognised in their report on trusts of land. The Commission recommended that all settlements should be established behind a trust unless a settlement were expressly and specifically created.

References

(1) (1883) 31 WR 912
(2) [1902] 1 Ch 378
(3) [1936] Ch 147
(4) [1947] 2 All ER 576

UNIVERSITY OF LONDON
LLB EXAMINATIONS 1994
for External Students
PART I EXAMINATION (Scheme A) and
SECOND AND THIRD YEAR EXAMINATIONS
(Scheme B)

LAND LAW

Monday, 6 June: 10.00 am to 1.00 pm

Answer *FOUR* of the following EIGHT questions

1 In 1989 Henry inherited some money from his grandfather and he and his girlfriend, Ann, decided to buy a house together. The purchase price of the house was £100,000. Henry contributed £80,000 and Ann contributed £20,000, a gift from her mother. The house was conveyed to them as beneficial joint tenants. In 1990 Ann gave birth to twins. In 1992 after a series of violent rows it became clear to both Henry and Ann that they could no longer live together and Henry agreed to move out. He wrote to her offering to sell her his interest in the house and she wrote back agreeing in principle to his proposal but pointing out that she would have to approach her mother for a loan. Shortly thereafter Henry was killed in a climbing accident leaving his entire estate to his brother, Paul. Paul now wants to sell the house and he requires Ann to pay an occupation rent pending sale. Ann has spent money on necessary repairs to the house and wishes to continue living there with her children.

Advise Ann.

2 Old Mrs Williams was persuaded ('for tax reasons') by her son, Jason, to sell him her house for £50,000 and Jason was duly registered as the proprietor. The purchase price was considerably less than the true value of the house, because Jason had agreed that his mother could stay in the house rent-free for the remainder of her life. Two years later Jason sold the house to David for £100,000, informing David falsely that he and his mother were intending to emigrate to Canada. David was registered as the proprietor of the house and Jason disappeared with the purchase money. David now seeks possession of the

house from Mrs Williams, while she claims that she is entitled to be registered as proprietor in his place.

Discuss.

3 In 1979 Miss Sprigg purchased Oaktree Cottage (registered land). The garden of the cottage backed on to a field from which it was separated by an old wooden fence. The field formed part of the Blackacre Estate whose owner, Lord Blacktown, intended to develop it as a caravan site for summer tourists. In 1980 Miss Sprigg removed part of the fence and began cultivating vegetables on part of the field; in 1981 she built a chicken coop on the field and reared chickens there; in 1982 she fenced in that part of the field that she was using to protect her chickens and vegetables from thieves and animals. In 1984 Miss Sprigg died leaving the cottage to her sister, Maud. Maud continued to grow vegetables and keep chickens on the enclosed part of the field. In 1991 Lord Blacktown sold the field to Sunshine Caravans and they wrote to Maud informing her that they proposed to develop the field as a caravan site and requiring her to vacate the field. Maud ignored the letter and in 1994 Sunshine Caravans commenced proceedings for possession.

Advise Maud.

4 Alex divided up his land (unregistered land) into four equal sized plots (Plots A, B, C and D) and built a substantial house on each of them. He decided to live on Plot A himself and he sold Plots B, C and D to Barry, Carol and Diana in that order. When they purchased their plots, Barry, Carol and Diana entered into identical covenants 'with Alex and his successors-in-title', covenanting (i) to use the house as a single dwelling-house, (ii) to use the house for residential purposes only, (iii) to maintain the house in a good state of repair. All four plots have since been sold: Plot A to Paul, Plot B to Quentin, Plot C to Rachel and Plot D to Stella. The house on Plot B has fallen into disrepair and Quentin proposes to divide the house into flats which he will sell. Rachel has started a massage business on Plot C. Paul and Stella want to enforce the covenants against Quentin and Rachel.

Advise them.

5 'In recent times the courts have so elevated the standard of conduct expected of the selling mortgagee that the mortgagee's duty to his mortgagor has become analogous to a fiduciary duty.'

Discuss.

6 In 1983 Smith granted Jones a lease of Whiteacre for a term of ten years and Jones covenanted to pay £6,000 per annum rent for the duration of the term and to maintain Whiteacre in a good state of decoration and repair. In 1985, Jones requested a licence to assign the lease to Arnold and a deed was made between Smith, Jones, Arnold and Arnold's surety, Paul, in which Smith granted the licence to assign and Arnold covenanted to pay the rent and observe the covenants in the lease. In 1990 Arnold assigned the residue of the term to Tim and Smith assigned his reversion to Robb. Since 1992 no rent has been paid and Whiteacre has fallen into disrepair.

Who has remedies against whom in request of these breaches of covenant?

Would your answer be different if the breaches had occurred after the term had been extended by statute in 1993?

7 Peter owned two adjacent shops which fronted directly on to a busy street. In one shop he sold arts and crafts and in the other he ran a café. On the outside wall of the café he affixed a notice advertising his arts and crafts shop. Behind the two shops there was a large yard belonging to Peter which backed on to a road. Deliveries for the shops were usually made to the yard and Peter parked his car there. In 1991, wishing to concentrate on his arts and crafts business, Peter leased the café to James for ten years. Initially Peter did not object to James using the yard for deliveries to the café or parking his van there, but early in 1994 differences arose between Peter and James, and Peter told James to stop using the yard. James retaliated by removing the advertising notice from the wall of the café.

Discuss.

Would your answer be different if Peter had conveyed the freehold reversion in the café to James in 1993?

8 'The principle that a term must be certain applies to all leases and tenancy agreements. A term must either be certain or uncertain. It cannot be partly certain because the tenant can determine it any time and partly uncertain because the landlord cannot determine it for an uncertain period.'

Explain this statement and indicate the ways in which statute has intervened to give effect to leases that would otherwise fall foul of this principle.

QUESTION 1

General Comment

An interesting question on co-ownership which gives students a good opportunity to display their knowledge of the subject matter. The key point to note is that despite the fact that the purchase money for the house has been provided in unequal shares it was conveyed to the purchasers as beneficial joint tenants.

Skeleton Solution

Co-ownership trust for sale ss34–36 LPA 1925.

Legal title on a joint tenancy.

Beneficial interest on a joint tenancy.

Principle of survivorship.

Severance of beneficial interest – notice in writing, *Burgess* v *Rawnsley*.

Section 30 LPA 1925 – application for order of sale – secondary trust – *Jones* v *Challenger*.

Suggested Solution

A trust for sale arises where there are concurrent interests in land (ie where more than one person holds interests in the land at the same time). Accordingly, the persons holding the interests are co-owners. Today, for all practical purposes, there are two types of co-ownership – joint tenancy and tenancy in common. In cases of co-ownership it is vital to distinguish between ownership at law and ownership in equity (ie beneficial ownership).

Since 1 January 1926, the legal estate in the case of co-owned land must be held on a joint tenancy (s1 Law of Property Act (LPA) 1925). Here the legal estate will be so held by Henry and Ann.

Although the legal estate must always be held on a joint tenancy the equitable interest can be held on either a joint tenancy or a tenancy in common. In determining how the equitable interest is held, the general rule is that a grant to two or more persons without words of severance (words in the grant which show that the tenants are each to take a distinct share in the property) creates a beneficial joint tenancy. To this general rule there are two qualifications. First, there are certain circumstances in which equity may presume that a tenancy in common was intended unless there is an express indication to the contrary. Secondly, a joint tenancy cannot exist without the presence of the four unities (time, title, interest and possession). On the facts there are no words of severance here. One of the circumstances in which equity may presume that a tenancy in common was intended is where, as here, the co-owners purchasing the property have put up the purchase money in unequal proportions. Here Henry and Ann have contributed £80,000 and £20,000 respectively to the cost of this £100,000 house. The presumption in such circumstances is that they intend to take interests in the property proportionate to their contributions. However, this presumption can be rebutted if there is an express indication to the contrary. Here there is such an indication – the house was conveyed to Henry and Ann 'as beneficial joint tenants'. Accordingly, on the facts the beneficial interest is held on a joint tenancy.

The aforementioned conclusions about the legal estate and the equitable interest can be represented diagrammatically as follows:

Legal Estate	Equitable Interest
H + A	H + A
Joint Tenancy	Joint Tenancy

One of the hallmarks of a joint tenancy is the principle of survivorship. On the death of one joint tenant his interest in the land passes to the other joint tenant by the right of survivorship. This right takes precedence over any disposition made by a joint tenant's will.

It is possible to sever the equitable joint tenancy without disturbing the joint tenancy of the legal estate. However, in view of the principle of survivorship such severance must be done during the joint tenants' lifetime. Severance is clearly relevant here because after Henry moves out he writes to Ann offering to sell her his interest and she writes back agreeing in principle to this proposal if she can borrow the necessary money. Severance can be effected in a variety of ways but on the facts it would be necessary to focus upon two in particular – notice in writing and course of dealing. By virtue of s36(2) LPA 1925 a joint tenancy can be severed by a joint tenant giving written notice to the other joint tenants.

Any form of written notice will suffice provided it is given to all the other joint tenants and it shows a sufficient wish to effect an immediate severance. Henry writing to Ann could be so regarded. Further, severance may be effected by a course of dealing. A course of conduct will be sufficient to sever a joint tenancy if it indicates a common intention between the joint tenants that the joint tenancy should be severed. In *Burgess* v *Rawnsley* (1) it was held that an oral agreement between two joint tenants was sufficient to evince an intention by them that the beneficial joint tenancy ought to be severed even though the agreement was unenforceable because of non-compliance with s40 LPA 1925. If the beneficial joint tenancy has been severed here a tenancy in common in equal shares will be created. On Henry's death, the legal title remains in Ann alone and if severance is deemed to have taken place (which henceforth is assumed) then Henry's share in the beneficial interest will pass to Paul.

Turning to Paul's desire to sell the house it is important to remember that as co-owned land is held on trust for sale there is a duty on the trustees (ie Ann) to sell subject to a power to postpone sale if exercised unanimously (see *Re Mayo* (2)). However, Ann does not want to sell because she wants to continue living in the house with her young children. Accordingly, Paul is likely to seek an order for sale from the court under s30 LPA 1925 (under this provision a court can 'make such order as it thinks fit' on an application by 'any person interested' in the property). Upon Paul's application for a s30 order for sale the court will look for any 'secondary' or 'collateral' purpose to the trust – that is any reason for the purchase of the house other than sale. Here there is such a secondary purpose – Henry and Ann bought the house to live in it together with any children they might have. Where the court finds the existence of a secondary purpose and where that purpose is still – as here – subsisting the court will not usually grant a sale order (see *Jones* v *Challenger* (3)). Accordingly, on the facts it is likely that the court will postpone a sale until Ann's children are much older – when they cease to be of school age.

Finally by virtue of s1(1) of the Law of Property (Joint Tenants) Act 1964 a survivor of a joint tenancy (Ann) shall in favour of any purchaser of the property be deemed to be solely and beneficially interested if she conveys as beneficial owner. One exception to this provision is a memorandum of severance endorsed on the conveyance. Accordingly, on the facts, Paul should endorse a memorandum of severance on the conveyance.

References

(1) [1975] Ch 429
(2) [1943] Ch 302
(3) [1961] 1 QB 176

QUESTION 2

General Comment

The question was probably a welcome one for many students because for the most part it deals with matters – proprietary estoppel, s70(1)(g) overriding interests – which are usually central aspects of most undergraduate land law courses. However, the tailpiece on rectification of the register may have caught some students out since this is an aspect of land registration which tends to receive only passing coverage in many undergraduate courses.

Skeleton Solution

Licences protected by estoppel or in equity – *Bannister* v *Bannister*.

Mirror principle – overriding interests (crack in the mirror) s70(1)(g) LRA 1925.

Enquiries of persons on the land – *Hodgson* v *Marks*.

When must a person be in occupation for the purposes of s70(1)(g)? – *Abbey National Building Society* v *Cann*.

Rectification of the register – s82 LRA 1925.

Suggested Solution

The question raises at least three main issues. First, what interest has Mrs Williams in the house after her son Jason is registered as proprietor? Secondly, has David purchased subject to Mrs Williams' interest? Thirdly, can David obtain possession – will Mrs Williams be able to obtain rectification of the register? These questions will be considered in turn.

Mrs Williams sold her home to her son for a price considerably less than its true value on the understanding that she could remain in it rent-free for the rest of her life. The facts are very similar to *Bannister* v *Bannister* (1). There, a woman who owned two cottages orally agreed to sell them on the basis that the purchaser would allow her to remain in one of them rent-free for so long as she wished. The conveyance made no mention of this undertaking. Subsequently, when the purchaser tried to get the woman out, the Court of Appeal held that it would be a fraud to disregard the oral trust of land and the woman was entitled under a constructive trust to a life interest determinable on her ceasing to reside in the cottage. There was a similar finding in *Re Sharpe* (2), where a constructive trust was found to enable an aunt who lent her nephew money to remain in the house until she was repaid. Subsequently, these cases were criticised mainly because the constructive trust was seen as too wide a remedy.

More recently reliance in such situations has been placed upon the doctrine of proprietary estoppel. This type of estoppel operates to prevent the revocation of a right affecting land which one party has been led by the other to believe to be permanent. For example, if A, the owner of land, allows B to spend money on that land or otherwise act to his detriment under an expectation created or encouraged by A that he will be allowed to remain on the land or acquire an interest in the land, then A will not be allowed to defeat that expectation and deny B's right to remain or to an interest in the land.

The courts have used the equitable doctrines of estoppel and the constructive trust to protect licensees where it would be contrary to justice to allow strict legal principles to be applied (in *Bannister* v *Bannister* the trust of land was not in writing as required by s53(1)(b) Law of Property Act (LPA) 1925.)

Here Mrs Williams was persuaded to sell the house to her son at an undervalue because Jason agreed that she could remain in it rent-free for the rest of her life. Accordingly, it seems that Mrs Williams has a licence which Jason would be estopped from denying during her lifetime.

Has David purchased subject to the interest of Mrs Williams? In this regard it is necessary to discuss s70(1)(g) of the Land Registration Act (LRA) 1925. The register is designed to operate as a mirror accurately reflecting the totality of estates and interests affecting the registered land. Overriding interests are an exception to this principle (the mirror principle). They are not entered on to the register, yet they bind the registered proprietor even though he may have no knowledge of them (a crack in the mirror!). Overriding interests are set out in s70(1) LRA 1925. The most controversial one is para (g) which deals with the right of a person in actual occupation. Mrs Williams will be claiming that she has a para (g) overriding interest. To succeed she has to show three things. First, her interest in the land must be proprietary in nature. Second, that she is in actual occupation. In this regard it was held by the House of Lords in *Abbey National Building Society* v *Cann* (3) that the relevant date for occupation in order to establish a right under para (g) was the date of completion of the transaction. Third, that no enquiry was made of her. A purchaser of registered land is required to inspect the premises and ask anyone in occupation the grounds on which they are there (see *Hodgson* v *Marks* (4)). It is not enough to ask the vendor alone, it must be the person 'in actual occupation' (see *Hodgson* v *Marks*). Here Mrs Williams has a proprietary interest in the house and she was in occupation before Jason sold the house to David. Further, David accepted Jason's explanation and he made no enquiry of Mrs Williams. Accordingly, he has bought the house subject to Mrs Williams' overriding interest protected by her occupation.

A purchaser can take free of an otherwise overriding interest if he makes 'enquiry' of the person who owns the interest and that interest is not disclosed.

Can David obtain possession of the house? In view of the protection of s70(1)(g) LRA 1925, Mrs Williams will be able to resist any claim by David for possession. The court will invariably decide that she has a licence by estoppel. David has failed to make the enquiry necessary under s70(1)(g) and he now has a property which he cannot occupy or sell at full vacant possession market value because of the absolute requirement that a purchaser of registered land must enquire of any person occupying the land, what their interest is.

Finally, will Mrs Williams be able to obtain rectification of the register? Section 82 of the Land Registration Act 1925 gives a wide discretion to rectify the register to both the court and the Registrar in order to correct mistakes. There are eight grounds for rectification, including fraud, mistake and consent (where all interested persons consent). Here Mrs Williams is not the victim of fraud or mistake nor, presumably, does David consent. She has received £50,000 from Jason and will probably be allowed by the court to remain in the house for as long as she wishes. Accordingly, she will not succeed in her claim to rectify the register.

References

(1) [1948] 2 All ER 133
(2) [1980] 1 WLR 219
(3) [1991] 1 AC 56
(4) [1971] Ch 892

QUESTION 3

General Comment

This question was probably not one of the more popular ones on the paper as adverse possession (with which the question is concerned) is an area of land law which tends not to feature significantly in student revision schedules.

Skeleton Solution

Meaning of adverse possession.

Section 15 Limitation Act 1980.

Significance of fencing.

Successive squatters – aggregation of periods of adverse possession by different owners.

Significance of communication from paper owner – *Buckinghamshire County Council* v *Moran*.

Registering a caution – s70(1)(f) Land Registration Act 1925.

What action should squatter take in face of possession proceedings?

Suggested Solution

Adverse possession, with which this question is concerned, means possession inconsistent with the title of the true owner. Section 15 of the Limitation Act 1980 sets a 12-year period for the recovery of land. It provides that 'No action shall be brought to recover land after the expiration of 12 years from the date on which the right of action accrued'. Here it will be necessary to consider the following main issues: (a) when did adverse possession by Miss Sprigg commence? (b) successive periods of adverse possession, ie that of Miss Sprigg first and then Maud; (c) the significance of the communication from Sunshine Caravans who bought the field from Lord Blacktown; and (d) what action Maud can take in the face of possession proceedings commenced by Sunshine Caravans? Each of these issues will be considered in turn.

In 1979, Miss Sprigg purchased Oaktree Cottage which is registered land. Evidence of title takes the form of a register and filed plan issued by the Land Registry which will mirror the documentary title prior to first registration. On the facts given, the registered title will include the back garden up to the adjoining field. When, in 1980, Miss Sprigg removed part of the fence and went onto part of the field to cultivate vegetables she went onto land beyond her registered title and began to treat it as her own. As previously mentioned, s15 Limitation Act 1980 provides that no action can be brought by the true owner to recover any land after the expiration of 12 years from the date on which the right of action accrued to the plaintiff or the person through whom he claims. Time begins to run as soon as (a) the owner has been dispossessed or has discontinued his possession; and (b) adverse possession has been taken by some other person. Miss Sprigg must have had an intention to exclude the owner as well as other people (see *Powell* v *McFarlane* (1)). Adverse possession is a question of fact in which circumstances such as the nature of the land and the way in which the land is enjoyed must be taken into account. In *Wallis's Cayton Bay Holiday Camp* v *Shell-Mex and BP Ltd* (2) Lord Denning said that just because some other person enters onto land and uses it for some seasonal purpose like growing vegetables was not adverse to the owner. Accordingly, on the facts it is doubtful, before the fencing in 1982, that acts sufficient to show and establish factual possession and an intention to possess to the exclusion of all others exist. Enclosure is the strongest possible evidence of adverse possession but it is not indispensable (see *Seddon* v *Smith* (3)). It is submitted therefore that on the facts time began to run in 1982.

In 1984, Miss Sprigg died leaving Oaktree Cottage to her sister Maud. If a squatter who has not barred the true owner sells the land he can give the purchaser a right to the land which is as good as his own. This rule also applies to devises or gifts of the land by the squatter. In each case the person taking the squatter's interest can add the squatter's period of possession to his own. Here, Maud can add Miss Sprigg's two-year adverse possession to her own.

Turning to the position of the paper owner, it would seem that 12 years have elapsed since 1982 when the fencing was carried out by Miss Sprigg. However, in 1991 – before 12 years had elapsed – Maud received a letter from Sunshine Caravans informing her that they propose to develop the field as a caravan site and requiring her to vacate the field. It must be shown that the claimant has accepted the assertion of the right by the paper owner and the mere assertion alone by the true paper owner of a claim to possession in land, contained in a letter sent to the squatter, is not sufficient to prevent the squatter obtaining title by adverse possession. Accordingly, if Maud continued to use the land in spite of her knowledge of Sunshine Caravans' intentions this would not be a bar to her continuing to acquire title by adverse possession, provided she maintained her intention to possess the land (see *Buckinghamshire County Council* v *Moran* (4)).

What action should Maud take in the face of the possession proceedings? If Maud is confident that she has established factual possession and intention she could defend the possession proceedings and assert her squatter's title. She is in possession and should not move off the land unless she is willing to do so. Sunshine Caravans may wish to settle the proceedings and purchase her interest in the land. Maud could consider registering a caution against first registration in respect of the additional land which is undoubtedly an unregistered title. If it were in fact registered her occupation would be an overriding interest protected by s70)(1)(f) Land Registration Act 1925. Maud could make application to the Land Registry for title to the land on the basis of her adverse possession. However, in view of the commencement of proceedings by Sunshine Caravans the Land Registry would not proceed with her application until the outcome of the court proceedings were known.

Finally, it is important to note the raison d'etre of the Limitation Act 1980. It is that those who go to sleep upon their claims should not be helped by the courts in recovering their property and that there should be an end to litigation.

References

(1) (1977) 38 P & CR 452
(2) [1975] QB 94
(3) (1877) 36 LT 168
(4) [1989] 2 All ER 225

QUESTION 4

General Comment

This is a question concerning the enforcement of freehold covenants against successors in title of the original parties. The biggest problem with the question concerns Stella. As with most problem questions on this topic the inclusion of a diagrammatical representation of the facts is advisable, not least because it should eliminate the possibility of a student confusing the various parties in the course of an answer.

Skeleton Solution

Definition of a covenant.

Distinguishing between positive and restrictive covenants.

Running of the burden to successors in title of the original covenantor – equity rules.

Running of the benefit to successors in title of original covenantee – equity rules – express annexation *Rogers* v *Hosegood*, statutory annexation – *Federated Homes Ltd* v *Mill Lodge Properties Ltd* and scheme of development.

Registration.

Suggested Solution

A covenant, in the context of real property law, is an agreement by deed whereby one party (the covenantor) promises with another party (the covenantee) that he will or will not engage in some stated activity in relation to a specified piece of land. The land owned by the covenantee will have the benefit of the covenant and that owned by the covenantor will have the burden. On the facts Alex, who owns Plot A, is the original covenantee and Barry, Carol and Diana who respectively bought Plots B, C and D are the original covenantors.

There are two kinds of freehold covenant – positive and negative. A positive covenant is one which obliges the owner to do something on his land (a work covenant, eg a covenant to fence) or to contribute money towards work to be done or services to be provided for the benefit of his land (a money covenant, eg a covenant to contribute towards the construction or maintenance of a private road). A restrictive covenant is one which restrains a landowner in some respect from the uninhibited use of his property, eg a covenant which prevents the covenantor from using his land for the purpose of conducting trade or business. On the facts, covenant (i) to use the house as a single dwelling-house is a restrictive one, covenant (ii) to use the house for residential purposes only is also a restrictive one and covenant (iii) to maintain the house in a good state of repair is a positive one.

On the facts, Alex has sold Plot A to Paul (assignee of original covenantee) and the three original covenantors Barry, Carol and Diana have sold their respective plots to Quentin, Rachel and Stella. These developments can be represented diagrammatically as follows:

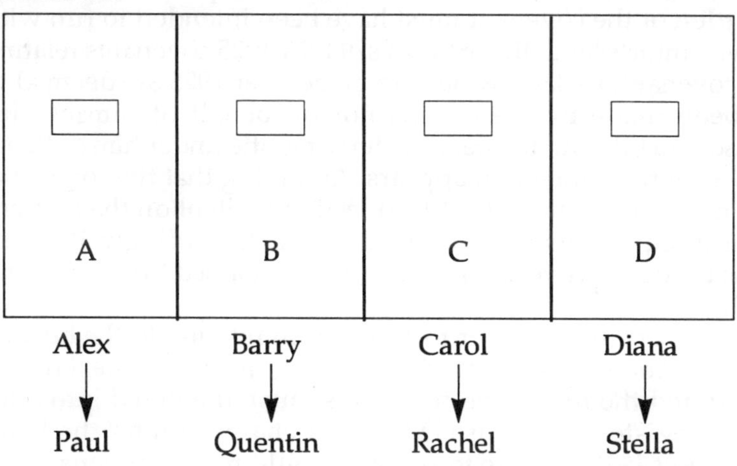

On the facts, Plot B is in disrepair (breach of covenant (iii)), Quentin is proposing to divide the house on Plot B into flats (breach of covenant (i)) and Rachel has started a massage business on Plot C (breach of covenants (i) and (ii)).

Paul and Stella want to enforce the three covenants against Quentin and Rachel. To do so they have to establish that the burden of the covenants has passed to Quentin and Rachel and that the benefit of the covenants has passed to them under either the common law or equity rules.

Turning first to the running of the burden of the covenants, the position at common law is that the the burden of a covenant, whether positive or negative, made between a vendor and purchaser cannot run directly with freehold land. This was laid down in *Austerberry* v *Corporation of Oldham* (1). Accordingly, it is necessary to consider whether the burden of the three covenants can run in equity. The burden of a covenant will only run in equity if three conditions are satisfied. First, the covenant must be a negative one. This was laid down in *Haywood* v *Brunswick Permanent Benefit Building Society* (2). It is enough if the covenant is negative in nature. Covenants (i) and (ii), as previously mentioned, are negative ones. Covenant (i) is negative in nature though worded positively. Since covenant (iii) is a positive one – it involves the spending of money – the burden cannot run either at law or in equity. Accordingly, Paul and Stella cannot enforce covenant (iii) against Quentin. Secondly, the covenant must have been made for the protection of land retained by the covenantee (Alex). The authority for this is *London County Council* v *Allen* (3). Both covenants (i) and (ii) would satisfy this requirement. Thirdly, the burden of the covenant must have been intended to run with the covenantor's land. By virtue of s79 LPA 1925 covenants relating to the covenantor's land which are made after 1925 are deemed to have been made by the covenantor on behalf of himself, his successors in title and the persons deriving title under him or them, unless a contrary intention appears. Assuming that the covenants were entered into after 1925 (the question is silent on the matter), this third requirement would be satisfied. Accordingly, it seems that the burden of covenants (i) and (ii) have passed to Quentin and Rachel.

There is one final matter to consider in relation to the burden of the covenants – registration. Where, as here, the land is unregistered the restrictive covenants must, if entered into after 1925, be registered as Class D (ii) land charges under the Land Charges Act 1972. Failure to register would render covenants (i) and (ii) void against a purchaser for value of a legal estate in the land (s4(6) Land Charges Act 1972).

Having shown that the burden of covenants (i) and (ii) can pass to Quentin and Rachel in equity it is now necessary for Paul and Stella to show that the benefit of these two covenants has passed to them. At common law the benefit of a covenant can run with freehold land if certain conditions are satisfied. However, since the burden of a covenant cannot run with freehold land directly at common law there is no real point in establishing if the benefit of covenants (i) and (ii) has passed to Paul and Stella at common law. Rather it is crucial to consider whether the benefit has passed to them in equity.

For the benefit of a restrictive covenant to pass in equity to a successor in title of the covenantee (Paul) the covenant must 'touch and concern' or 'benefit' some land of the covenantee and the benefit must be transmitted in one or more of the ways prescribed by equity (annexation, assignment or scheme of development). Here covenants (i) and (ii) touch and concern Plot A. The key issue is whether the benefit has passed to Paul and Stella in one or more of the ways recognised by equity.

In relation to Paul, it is necessary to consider annexation. Express annexation confers the benefit of the covenant upon the land and not individuals. Whether the benefit is so annexed to the land depends upon the wording of the covenants. In particular it must be possible to identify the land to be benefited from such wording. In *Rogers* v *Hosegood* (4) the covenant was deemed to be annexed since it referred to the dominant land. However, in *Renals* v *Cowlishaw* (5) the covenant was not annexed because it only referred to 'the vendors, their heirs, executors, administrators and assigns' (ie no reference was made to any land). Here the covenants were made 'with Alex and his successors in title'. This would not be enough for express annexation because there is no real identification of the benefited land.

However, statutory annexation is likely to be of help to Paul. In *Federated Homes Ltd* v *Mill Lodge Properties Ltd* (6) the Court of Appeal held that where a restrictive covenant touches and concerns the covenantee's land, s78(1) LPA 1925 annexes the benefit of the covenant to the covenantee's land and the covenant is enforceable at the suit of the covenantee and his successors in title. On the strength of *Federated Homes* it would seem that Paul could show that the benefit of covenants (i) and (ii) have passed to him. However, it is important to note that while the decision in *Federated Homes* was good news for conveyancers (s78 could come to the rescue if the express annexation formula used by them turned out to be deficient) the reasoning used by the Court of Appeal on that occasion is not beyond criticism. Accordingly, provided Paul can show statutory annexation (which seems likely) he will be able to enforce covenant (i) against Quentin and covenants (i) and (ii) against Rachel.

For Stella to be able to enforce covenants (i) and (ii) against Quentin and Rachel she would have to show that the land is subject to a scheme of development – not an impossible task given that Alex divided up the land into four equal-sized plots. The requirements for a scheme of development were first laid down in *Elliston* v *Reacher* (7). Today it seems that for such a scheme to exist two requirements have to be satisfied. First, the area of the scheme must be defined. Secondly, those who purchase from the creator of the scheme do so on the footing that all purchasers should be mutually bound by and mutually entitled to enforce a defined set of restrictions. Clearly, if a scheme of development can be established it could be pleaded by Paul, together with statutory annexation.

Assuming that Paul and Stella can show that the benefit of covenants (i) and (ii) has passed to them in equity and that the burden has passed to Quentin and Rachel in equity, the remedy that they would seek to stop Quentin dividing the house on Plot B into flats and to stop Rachel's massage business on Plot C would be an injunction.

References

(1) (1885) 29 Ch D 750
(2) (1881) 8 QBD 403
(3) [1914] 3 KB 642
(4) [1900] 2 Ch 388
(5) (1879) 11 Ch D 866
(6) [1980] 1 WLR 594
(7) [1908] 2 Ch 374

QUESTION 5

General Comment

A somewhat challenging essay title because of its specific focus, which would give a student well versed in the relevant law a good opportunity to exhibit his knowledge and understanding. Not a question to be undertaken by a student with only an outline understanding of the relevant law.

Skeleton Solution

Definition of a mortgage.

Power of sale – arising.

Power of sale – exercisable.

Mortgagee not a trustee of the power of sale.

Duty to mortgagor to take reasonable care – *Cuckmere Brick Co Ltd* v *Mutual Finance.*

Parker-Tweedale v *Dunbar Bank plc (No 1).*

Sale by mortgagee to himself – *Tse Kwong Lam* v *Wong Chit Sen*

Section 13 Building Societies Act 1986.

Section 105 LPA 1925.

Suggested Solution

A mortgage is essentially a transaction whereby an interest in property, be it land, house or business, is transferred to a mortgagee (lender) as security for the loan, subject to a right of redemption vested in the mortgagor (borrower).

The most important rights enabling the mortgagee to recover the capital sum and/or interest are taking possession, sale, foreclosure and appointing a receiver. The question concerns the power of sale which is the remedy most commonly used as it enables a mortgagee to recover his capital speedily. It is usually combined with an action to obtain vacant possession to allow the best price to be obtained.

The power of sale arises when the mortgage has been made by deed and the legal date of redemption has passed and there is no contrary intention expressed in the mortgage deed (s101 Law of

Property Act (LPA) 1925). Once the power of sale has arisen it becomes exercisable when one or more of the following conditions have been fulfilled: (i) default for three months after notice; or (ii) interest two months in arrear; or (iii) breach of some other term of the mortgage (s103 LPA 1925). The statutory power of sale is exercisable without a court order.

Over the last 25 years the responsibilities of a mortgagee to a mortgagor when selling mortgaged property have been considered by the courts on a number of occasions. In the first place it is important to note that a mortgagee has an absolute discretion as to the mode and time of sale. It can choose to sell by way of private treaty or by way of auction and it is not required to wait until the market improves. Further, the mortgagee's motive for selling – spite against the mortgagor – has been held immaterial (see *Nash* v *Eads* (1).

However, once the mortgagee decides to sell it is subject to certain duties. First and foremost, it was laid down in *Cuckmere Brick Co Ltd* v *Mutual Finance Ltd* (2) that a mortgagee is not a trustee for the mortgagor in respect of the power of sale because the power is given to the mortgagee for his own benefit to enable him the better to realise his security.

However, the mortgagor is the person interested in the proceeds of sale in so far as they exceed the mortgage debt, and his interests must not be sacrificed. Accordingly, a mortgagee is under some duty to the mortgagor with regard to the sale. Originally the duty was considered to be no more than a duty to act in good faith (see *Kennedy* v *De Trafford* (3)). However, since the early 1970s it has been recognised that more than good faith is required. In the landmark case of *Cuckmere Brick Co Ltd* v *Mutual Finance Ltd* it was held that the mortgagee owes the mortgagor a duty to take reasonable care. There the mortgagee advertised the property for sale by auction but omitted to mention a valuable planning permission. Salmon LJ stated that the mortgagee was under a duty to take reasonable precautions to obtain the true market value of the mortgaged property at the date when the mortgagee decides to sell. In *Standard Chartered Bank* v *Walker* (4) the Court of Appeal held that this duty was owed not only to the mortgagor but also to any guarantor of the mortgagor's debt. Any breach of this duty of care will render the mortgagee liable to the mortgagor for the difference between the price obtained and the price that he could have obtained. Where the mortgagee is a building society s13(7) and Schedule 4 para 1(1)(a) of the Building Societies Act 1986 requires the selling building society to achieve 'the best price that can reasonably be obtained'.

In *Parker-Tweedale* v *Dunbar Bank plc (No 1)* (5) the Court of Appeal further considered this duty of care owed by a mortgagee to a mortgagor. The court stated that the duty arose in equity and not in negligence. Accordingly, it did not give rise to liability against third parties. There the duty of care did not extend to the beneficiary under a trust of which the mortgagor was a trustee.

A sale by the mortgagee to himself either directly or through a third party may be set aside. In *Tse Kwong Lam* v *Wong Chit Sen* (6) the matter was considered by the Privy Council. There it was held that there was no inflexible rule that a mortgagee exercising his power of sale under a mortgage could not sell to a company in which he had an interest. However, the mortgagee and the company had to show that the sale was made in good faith and that the mortgagee had taken reasonable precautions to obtain the best price reasonably obtainable at the time.

After paying off all prior mortgages, the money received from the purchase is held by the mortgagee on trust. This money must be used by the mortgagee, in the following order, to: (i) pay all expenses incidental to the sale; (ii) pay himself the principal, interest and costs due under the mortgage; and (iii) pay the surplus, if any, to the next mortgagee, or if none, to the mortgagor (see s105 LPA 1925). If there is a subsequent mortgagee he will hold the balance on trust to discharge the money owing to him and to pay the balance to the person next entitled.

The question of the mortgagee's responsibilities on sale to the mortgagor is an area of land law which has seen considerable development over the last 25 years. It is now clear that more than good faith is entailed. Rather, it is now clearly established that the mortgagee owes to the mortgagor a duty to take reasonable care. Given the view of the Court of Appeal in *Parker-Tweedale* v *Dunbar Bank plc (No 1)* that the mortgagee's duty arises in equity and not in negligence it is true to say that the duty is now analogous to a fiduciary one.

References

(1) (1880) 25 SJ 95

(2) [1971] Ch 949 – 698

(3) [1897] AC 180

(4) [1982] 1 WLR 1410

(5) [1990] 3 WLR 767

(6) [1983] 3 All ER 54

QUESTION 6

General Comment

A question on the enforceability of leasehold covenants covering privity of contract and estate. In the main a well-prepared student should have had no real difficulty in coping with most of the points raised. However, asking for a licence to assign in 1985 (presumably because the lease so required) but not in 1990 was likely to have puzzled many students, as it did the writer.

Skeleton Solution

Privity of contract. Privity of estate.

Covenants which touch and concern.

Breaches subsequent to assignment of reversion – S no right to sue.

Benefit passes to R – s141 LPA 1925

J liable as original covenantor throughout the term.

If J has to pay can he recover from A, A's surety or T? *Moule* v *Garrett, P & A Swift Investments* v *Combined English Stores Group.*

T liable to R on the basis of privity of estate.

Statutory extension – *City of London Corporation* v *Fell.*

Suggested Solution

At the outset it is necessary to explain the concepts of privity of contract, privity of estate and touching and concerning which are central to dealing with this question on leases. As between the original landlord (S) and the original tenant (J) there is privity of contract. This contractual liability subsists throughout the whole term of the lease unless J is excused by the terms of the lease or of the licence to assign. Where there is privity of contract all covenants in the lease are enforceable. Privity of estate exists where the relationship of landlord and tenant exists between the parties. If L grants a lease to T and then T assigns it to A, there is no privity of contract between L and A because there has been no direct transaction between them. There is, however, privity of estate because A has acquired the estate which was created by L. Here there is privity of estate between R and T. Where there is privity of estate the benefit of the tenant's covenants and the burden of the landlord's covenants run with the reversion and the benefit of the landlord's covenants and the burden of the tenant's covenants run with the lease. However, in each case the doctrine of privity of estate only applies to covenants which 'touch and concern' the land. A covenant touches and concerns land if it affects the landlord as landlord or the tenant as tenant (ie it is not a personal one). Here the covenant to pay rent and the covenant to maintain Whiteacre in a good state of decoration and repair both touch and concern the land.

In 1983, S granted J a 10-year lease of Whiteacre. In 1985, J asked for a licence to assign – presumably because the lease so required. What is puzzling is why the parties did not need another licence to assign in 1990 when A assigned to T and if so why S did not follow his earlier precedent and demand a fresh covenant from T. Also in 1990, S assigned his reversion to R. These developments can be represented diagrammatically as follows:

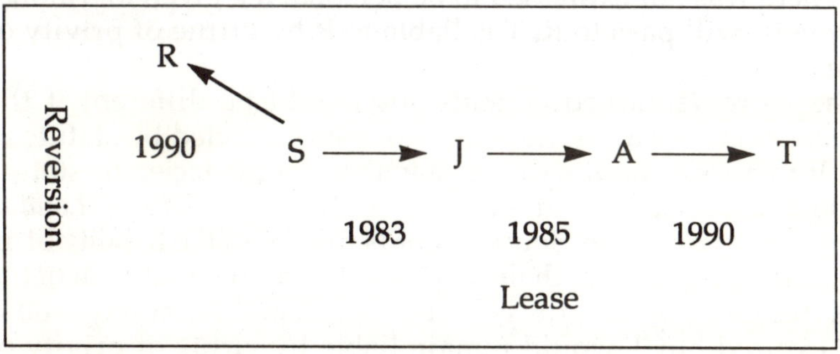

The breaches of covenant date from 1992, ie they did not take place until after S assigned his reversion to R. Accordingly, S has no interest and no right to sue for breach. By s141 Law of Property Act (LPA) 1925 the benefit of all covenants 'having reference to the subject matter' of the lease pass with the reversion to the assignee. Accordingly, the benefit passes to R who is thus the prospective plaintiff.

As previously mentioned, J as original covenantor remains liable on the two covenants throughout the 10-year term unless excused by the terms of the lease or of the licence to assign. Where a legal lease is assigned and thereafter a breach of covenant occurs the landlord can sue either the tenant on the basis of privity of contract or the assignee on the basis of privity of estate. Although in these circumstances the landlord has a choice as to who to sue he cannot obtain a double satisfaction. Here, if J is called upon to pay he would have an indemnity against A by virtue of s77(1)(c) LPA 1925, which provides for a covenant of indemnity to be implied into every assignment for value. Further, J would have an indemnity against A's surety or in quasi-contract against T (see *Moule* v *Garrett* (1)).

By entering into express covenants to pay rent and observe the covenants in the lease, A has put himself in the same position as the original covenantor J and he remains liable on the covenants throughout the rest of the term unless excused by the terms of the 1985 licence to assign. By virtue of s77(1)(c) LPA 1925 A has an implied right of indemnity against T. Paul, A's surety, incurs similar liability as original covenantor. This is because of the House of Lords' decision in *P & A Swift Investments* v *Combined English Stores Group* (2). There their Lordships held that the benefit of a surety covenant could run with the reversion if the surety guaranteed performance of the tenant's covenants, which themselves touched and concerned the land. So long as the surety given here was not expressed to be personal (eg given to S alone) the benefit will pass to R. T is liable to R by virtue of privity of estate.

The aforementioned conclusions would be different if the breaches occurred after the term had been extended by statute in 1993. If there is a statutory extension then, prima facie, the statute extends the tenancy but not the contract. In *City of London Corporation* v *Fell* (3) the House of Lords ruled that the liability of an original tenant ceased with the expiry of the contractual term of the lease. Accordingly, here the liabilities of J, A and A's surety would have expired but T would remain liable by virtue of privity of estate.

Finally, it is worth noting that the rule that the original lessor and original lessee remain liable on the covenants throughout the term of the lease, even after respectively assigning the reversion or lease, is a controversial one and has led to proposals for its abolition (4).

References

(1) (1872) LR 7 Ex 101
(2) [1988] 2 All ER 885
(3) [1993] 3 WLR 1164
(4) 1988 Law Com No 174

QUESTION 7

General Comment

A somewhat deceptive question. At first sight it seems to be a fairly straightforward question on easements but the more you get into it the more issues that emerge. A thorough understanding of the relevant methods of acquiring an easement is essential in order to tackle this question.

Skeleton Solution

Characteristics of an easement.

Implied grant – common intention – *Pwllbach Colliery Co Ltd* v *Woodman*.

Easement of car parking – *London and Blenheim Estates Ltd* v *Ladbroke Retail Parks Ltd*.

Bare licence.

Voluntary waste.

Implied grant – s62 LPA 1925.

Easement to have a sign on neighbouring property – *Moody* v *Steggles*.

Reservation.

Suggested Solution

An easement is a right in or over the land of another. In order to be an easement the right in question must satisfy the following characteristics (see *Re Ellenborough Park* (1)): (i) there must be a dominant and servient tenement; (ii) the easement must accommodate the dominant tenement; (iii) the dominant and servient tenements must not be both owned and occupied by the same person; (iv) a right over land cannot amount to an easement unless it is capable of forming the subject matter of a grant; and (v) the right must be against other land (ie it is not a right to possession of other land). James' claim to use the yard behind the two shops for deliveries is a claim to a right of way which will satisfy the aforementioned characteristics of an easement.

In order for a right to be an easement, not only must it satisfy the characteristics of an easement, it must also be properly acquired as an easement. There are a variety of ways in which an easement can be acquired. On the facts, assuming the 1991 lease of the café by Peter to James is silent on the matter, the issue is whether there is an implied grant to James of a right to use the yard for deliveries. There are a variety of ways in which a grant of an easement may be implied in favour of a purchaser/lessee of land.

The first is necessity where the implied grant is necessary to prevent land-locking. In *Titchmarsh* v *Royston Water Co Ltd* (2) it was held that the availability of an alternative route enjoyable as of right was destructive of any claim of necessity, even though the alternative route was inconvenient. Here there is no easement of necessity because it is possible to make deliveries to the café via the busy road onto which it fronts.

The second is s62 Law of Property Act (LPA) 1925, by virtue of which unless a contrary intention appears every conveyance of land passes with it all easements 'appertaining or reputed to appertain to the land ... or at the time of the conveyance occupied or enjoyed with the land ...' However, for s62 to be available there must have been some diversity of ownership or occupation of the quasi-dominant and quasi-servient tenements prior to the conveyance (see *Sovmots Investments Ltd* v *Secretary of State for the Environment* (3)). Given that prior to the 1991 lease the arts and crafts shop and the café were in Peter's sole ownership and occupation, s62 is not available because of no diversity of ownership or occupation.

The third is the doctrine of *Wheeldon* v *Burrows* (4). Under this doctrine, on the grant of part of a tenement there passes to the grantee, as easements, all quasi-easements which were continuous and apparent and were used by the grantor for the benefit of the part granted. 'Apparent' means capable of discovery by careful inspection of the land. On the facts the doctrine would not be available as the right being claimed by James is unlikely to be apparent. Finally, in relation to implied grant there are intended easements. These are easements necessary to carry out the clear common intention of the parties (see *Pwllbach Colliery Co Ltd* v *Woodman* (5)). It may be that an easement of way could be inferred on the basis of the common intention of Peter and James.

As to James' claim to park his van in the yard at the back of the shops, it is now clear that there can be an easement to park provided that exclusive occupation of the servient land is not given (see *London & Blenheim Estates Ltd* v *Ladbroke Retail Park Ltd* (6)). However, there seems to be no basis for implying the grant of a right to park a van here. Accordingly, it seems that on the facts James parks by virtue of a bare licence which can be revoked by the licensor at any time provided he gives the licensee reasonable notice. Further, there is nothing on the facts to raise an estoppel as in *Ives Investments Ltd* v *High* (7).

Peter telling James to stop using the yard constitutes an infringement of James' right to enjoy what seems to be an established easement. However, such infringement does not entitle James to take retaliatory action by way of removing the advertising notice from the wall of the café. On the facts James' removal of the shop-sign is an act of voluntary waste (a positive act which damages the land) by a tenant for which he may, subject to the terms of the lease, be held liable.

A conveyance of the freehold reversion in the café to James in 1993 would affect the above conclusions in several respects. Subject to any relevant provisions in the conveyance, James could claim an implied right to use the yard for deliveries as before. However, the parking of his van hitherto by way of licence would now be by an easement by virtue of s62 LPA 1925 provided the extent of the right claimed does not amount to a claim to possession of part of the servient land.

Finally, if James was the freehold owner of the café he could remove the notice advertising the arts and crafts shop unless prevented by some counter-right in Peter. It is questionable whether Peter could establish any such right. In *Moody* v *Steggles* (8) it was held that right to fix a sign board on a neighbouring house could be an easement. However, on the facts it is necessary to ask whether this right accommodates Peter's land or merely his business (see *Hill* v *Tupper* (9)). In any event was any such right ever granted? If it was it would have to be by way of an express reservation in the 1993 conveyance as there is no necessity and insufficient evidence of common intention.

References

(1) [1956] Ch 131
(2) (1899) 81 LT 673
(3) [1977] AC 144
(4) (1879) 12 Ch D 31
(5) [1915] AC 634
(6) [1992] 1 WLR 1278
(7) [1967] 2 QB 379
(8) (1879) 12 Ch D 261
(9) (1863) 2 H & C 121

QUESTION 8

General Comment

Determining what this unattributed statement actually means as a matter of plain English is not without difficulty. However, the writer has assumed that the central issue is the *Lace* v *Chantler* point that the duration of a lease must be certain. The question provides students well-versed with this essential requirement for a valid lease and the related statutory provisions with a fairly straightforward opportunity to display their knowledge and understanding.

Skeleton Solution

Essential requirements of a lease.

Term or duration must be certain – *Lace* v *Chantler.*

Ashburn Anstalt v *Arnold.*

Prudential Assurance Co Ltd v *London Residuary Body.*

Periodic tenancies.

Leases for lives – s149(6) LPA 1925.

Leases for perpetuity – s145 LPA 1922.

Suggested Solution

Since 1 January 1926, there are only two estates which are capable of existing at law: the fee simple absolute in possession and the term of years absolute or lease (see s1(1) Law of Property Act (LPA) 1925). For there to be a valid legal lease four requirements must be satisfied. First, the premises must be sufficiently defined. Secondly, the tenant must have been granted exclusive possession of the property, ie the tenant can exclude everyone including the landlord from the property for the duration of the term. Thirdly, both the commencement date and the duration of the term must be certain or capable of being ascertained at the outset of the term (see s205(1)(xxvii) LPA 1925). Fourthly, any relevant formalities must be complied with. For example, a lease in excess of three years must be granted by deed (see ss52(1) and 54(2) LPA 1925). This question concerns the third requirement.

In order for a lease for a fixed term to be valid it must have a certain duration. In *Lace* v *Chantler* (1) a lease granted during the course of the Second World War for the duration of the war was void. However, several Court of Appeal decisions in recent years cast some doubt on this principle. For example, *Re Midland Railway Company's Agreement* (2) decided that the landlord could bar himself from determining the lease. This case was applied by the Court of Appeal in *Ashburn Anstalt* v *Arnold* (3). However, the principle of *Lace* v *Chantler* was reaffirmed by the House of Lords in *Prudential Assurance Co Ltd* v *London Residuary Body* (4). There their Lordships held that a lease 'until land was required for widening the road' was void because the period was uncertain. Lord Templeman said of *Re Midland Railway Company's Agreement* that if it was correctly decided it would make it unnecessary for a lease to be of a certain duration. However, their Lordships held that it had been wrongly decided and it was overruled (*Ashburn Anstalt* v *Arnold* was also overruled on this point).

The rule that a lease must be certain or capable of being made certain at the outset of the term applies also to periodic tenancies (tenancies from month-to-month, year-to-year etc). In *Prudential Assurance Co Ltd* v *London Residuary Body*, Lord Templeman explained how a yearly periodic tenancy could be certain. He said that

> 'a tenancy from year- to-year is saved from being uncertain because each party has power by notice to determine at the end of any year. The term continues until determined as if both parties made a new agreement at the end of each year for a new term for the ensuing year' (5).

Accordingly, *Prudential Assurance Co Ltd* v *London Residuary Body* has brought about a welcome return to orthodoxy.

The requirement that the commencement date and duration of the term must be certain for a lease to be valid would mean that a lease for life and a lease for perpetuity would both fall foul of this principle and be void. However, in respect of both types of lease statute has intervened to prevent this happening. By virtue of s149(6) LPA 1925 leases at a rent for life or lives or until the marriage of the lessee are converted into leases for a term of 90 years determinable after the end of the life or lives or on the marriage of the lessee, as the case may be, by the giving by either party of not less than one month's notice expiring on one of the quarter days, applicable to the tenancy. It is important to note that this provision only applies to a lease at a rent or fine. A term determinable with life at no rent may come within s20(1)(iv) Settled

Land Act 1925 and so create a strict settlement (see *Ungurian* v *Lesnoff* (6)).

A perpetually renewable lease is one which gives the lessee the right to renew the lease for another period as often as it expires. They are converted by s145 and Schedule 15 LPA 1922 into terms of 2,000 years determinable only by the lessee by not less than ten days' notice expiring on any of the old renewal dates. Basically, if the covenant for renewal is part of a separate obligation then there is no perpetually renewable lease (see *Marjorie Burnett* v *Barclay* (7)). However, if the lease is to be renewed on the existing terms, including the covenant for renewal, then there will be a perpetually renewable lease (see *Parkus* v *Greenwood* (8)).

Finally, for a lease to be valid its duration must be certain in the sense that there is either a definite limit to the length of the term (period fixed at the outset) or the limit can be set by either party in a clearly defined way (periodic tenancy).

References

(1) [1944] KB 368
(2) [1971] Ch 725
(3) [1989] Ch 1
(4) [1992] 3 WLR 279
(5) Ibid at p 285
(6) [1989] 3 WLR 840
(7) (1980) 258 EG 642 360
(8) [1950] Ch 644

UNIVERSITY OF LONDON
LLB EXAMINATIONS 1995
for External Students
PART I EXAMINATION (Scheme A) and
SECOND AND THIRD YEAR EXAMINATIONS (Scheme B)

LAND LAW

Thursday, 8 June: 10.00 am to 1.00 pm

Answer *FOUR* of the following EIGHT questions

1 'The law of forfeiture has become unnecessarily complicated, is no longer coherent and gives rise to injustices.'

With reference to this statement, discuss the principal shortcomings of the law relating to the forfeiture of leases and consider ways in which it should be reformed.

2 Jack Bird had one son, Paul, who had emigrated to Australia, and two nieces, Frances and Grace. When, in 1988, Frances told him about her plans to raise poultry, Jack offered her the use of an unoccupied cottage he owned in the country. 'You are welcome to use it,' he said, 'it needs quite a lot doing to it to make it habitable, but you don't need to pay me any rent.' Frances and her boyfriend moved into the cottage, made it habitable and embarked on their poultry business. In 1989 Grace lost her job and Jack suggested that she should go and live with him in his London house and assist him as unpaid housekeeper and secretary. In 1992, at a time when Jack was ill, he told Grace not to worry about the future as he was leaving her the London house in his will. In 1994 Jack retired, sold the house and bought a bungalow by the sea. Jack and Grace lived in the bungalow for two months until his death later the same year. In his will Jack left his whole estate to his son, Paul, who now seeks possession of both the cottage and the bungalow.

Advise Frances and Grace.

3 In 1970 Bob, a builder, asked his friend and neighbour, Frank, a farmer, whether he could store his building materials

somewhere on Frank's land. Frank agreed, 'Of course. You can use that old shed adjoining your land. It is virtually empty and I have no immediate use for it.' Bob has used the shed for his materials ever since and on two occasions, in 1976 and in 1986, he reroofed the shed to keep it waterproof. In 1977 Frank sold his farm to Gus. Gus never objected to Bob's use of the shed and he never used the shed for his own purposes, though he thought that the shed might be useful in the future if he started a market garden on his land. In 1994 Gus sold his land to Spike. Spike has now refused to allow Bob to enter the shed.

Discuss.

4 'There is now no rule in equity which precludes a mortgagee ... from stipulating for any collateral advantage.' (Per Lord Parker of Waddington).

Explain this statement and consider the circumstances in which the courts will still be prepared to strike down collateral advantages.

5 Alfred was the owner of a piece of undeveloped land (unregistered land) and in 1980 he decided to divide it into three plots, each of them fronting on to the highway, and to build a substantial house on each plot. He decided to live in the house built on the central plot, plot B. He sold plot A in fee simple to Vince, who covenanted with Alfred and his successors-in-title to use the house for residential purposes only and to maintain the garden and the dividing wall in good condition. Alfred for his part covenanted with Vince and his successors-in-title to use his house for residential purposes only and to maintain the garden on plot B in good condition. A year later Alfred leased plot C to Larry for a term of 99 years, Larry covenanting to use the house for residential purposes only and to maintain the garden and the dividing wall in good condition.

Mary, who purchased plot B in 1983, would like to know whether she can enforce the covenants against Pete, who has recently purchased plot A from Vince and against Quentin, who has recently taken an assignment of Larry's lease.

Advise.

6 After the death of her husband, Brenda decided to go to London to live with her three unmarried daughters, Iris, Jill and Kirsten. Brenda purchased a large house for them all and, although she paid the whole purchase price, she agreed that it should be conveyed into the names of her daughters as beneficial joint tenants. It was understood that Brenda would live in the

'granny flat' in the basement for the rest of her life. Two years later Iris got married and moved out of the house; Jill and Kirsten agreed to buy her interest in the house but Iris was killed in a car accident before anything further was done. Jill has now been posted abroad and has suggested that the house should be sold. Brenda resists this suggestion.

Discuss. If the house were sold, how would the proceeds be divided?

7 When Tim married Janet, Barbara, Tim's mother, bought a house for the couple to live in. Barbara paid the whole of the purchase price and the house was registered in her sole name. The couple agreed to be responsible for repairs and other outgoings and they insisted, against Barbara's wishes, on paying her a token monthly 'rent'. A few years later the marriage broke down and Tim moved out of the house. Janet continued living in the house, doing the repairs and paying the rent. Finding herself short of cash, Barbara decided to sell the house and, while Janet was away on holiday, she sold it to a local building company. As the new registered proprietor, the company seeks possession of the house with a view to redeveloping the site.

Advise Janet.

8 Consider the effect of the following dispositions:

a) a conveyance of Blackacre to Alice in fee simple for as long as she lives on Blackacre;

b) a lease of Whiteacre at a rent to Bert for twenty-five years or Bert's life, whichever shall be the shorter period;

c) a lease of Greenacre to Calum at a weekly rent to determine on the day of the next General Election.

QUESTION 1

General Comment

A particularly challenging essay title. It would not be enough to simply outline the law of forfeiture in relation to leases. An answer must identify the main shortcomings of the current law. Further, a good answer would include coverage of the recent Law Commission proposals for reform of this area of law.

Skeleton Solution

Determination of leases.

Forfeiture for non-payment of rent.

Forfeiture for breach of covenants other than rent.

Position of lesser interest holders.

Waiver.

Main problems with the current law.

Law Commission Report on Forfeiture of Tenancies 1985.

Law Commission Termination of Tenancies Bill 1994.

Suggested Solution

There are several ways in which a lease may come to an end, of which forfeiture is one (others include effluxion of time and merger of the reversion and the lease). Forfeiture involves the landlord bringing a lease to a premature end because of serious default on the part of the tenant. A landlord has an implied right to forfeit for breach of a condition. However, he may only forfeit a lease for breach of covenant if there is an express forfeiture clause in the lease (ie he has stipulated for it). Every well-drafted lease will contain an express forfeiture clause. Forfeiture may be effected either by serving a writ for possession, or by peaceable re-entry. However, if the premises are a dwelling house the landlord must secure a court order.

The procedure to be followed to effect a forfeiture differs depending upon whether forfeiture is being sought for (i) non-payment of rent, or (ii) breach of other covenants in the lease. In the ensuing paragraphs an outline of both procedures is given.

In the case of non-payment of rent, the landlord must make a formal demand (ie he or his agent must demand the exact sum due in the demised premises on the day it is due at such convenient hour before sunset as will give time to count out the money) unless excused from doing so. This requirement can be dispensed with if expressly excluded by the lease (which it is in all standard form leases). Further, the need for a formal demand can also be dispensed with if the rent is more than six months in arrears and there are insufficient goods available for distress on the premises to satisfy the arrears (s210 Common Law Procedure Act 1852). The landlord's right to forfeit for non-payment of rent is regarded merely as a security for the sum due. Accordingly, if a landlord brings an action for possession the tenant has the right to have the action discontinued if he pays all arrears and costs at any time before the trial (s212 Common Law Procedure Act 1852). The court can give a tenant relief from forfeiture (ie restore the tenant to his lease) even after judgment. The power to do so was originally equitable but is now regulated by statute (ss210–212 Common Law Procedure Act 1852). The tenant must apply within six months of the judgment and relief will be granted if he pays the rent due and the landlord's costs, and if it is equitable in the circumstances to grant relief. It is important to note that granting relief is a matter for the discretion of the court. If, however, the landlord has re-let the premises relief will not be granted: *Stanhope* v *Howarth* (1). Where the head tenancy is forfeit for non-payment of rent a sub-tenant can seek relief from forfeiture under s146(4) Law of Property Act (LPA) 1925.

If a landlord wishes to forfeit for a breach of some covenant other than rent he must observe a different procedure. He must serve a written notice on the tenant under s146 LPA 1925 and the notice must specify the nature of the breach, demand it to be remedied and, if possible, require the tenant to pay compensation for the breach (unless the landlord chooses to waive this). The landlord must give the tenant a reasonable time to comply with the notice. What is a reasonable time depends on the nature of the breach. Three months is usually considered reasonable. If the breach is irremediable only a short period of time need be given to the tenant (a week or two, to enable the tenant to seek legal advice) before the landlord commences proceedings. A breach of a covenant against assignment or sub-letting would be irremediable (*Scala House & District Property Co Ltd* v *Forbes* (2)). The tenant may apply for relief against forfeiture. Section 146(2) LPA 1925 gives the court a wide discretion to allow the tenant relief on terms that the breach of covenant ceases. In the case of an irremediable breach the court will not allow relief from forfeiture. Nor will relief be allowed if the landlord has already re-entered. Finally, a sub-tenant or mortgagee of the tenant may also apply for relief because if the lease is forfeited any sub-lease or mortgage falls with it.

A landlord may lose his right to forfeit by waiving the breach of covenant. Waiver can be express or implied. An implied waiver will arise if the landlord, knowing of the tenant's breach, does some act which unequivocally shows that he regards the lease as still continuing. The most typical act of waiver is the demand and acceptance of rent. However, it is a question of fact whether or not the landlord has waived the breach of covenant.

The law of forfeiture of leases has a number of shortcomings. The Law Commission has described the current law as 'complex and confused' (3). A number of reasons can be advanced in support of such a conclusion. First, the fact that there are separate procedures depending upon whether the landlord is proposing to forfeit for non-payment of rent or for breach of some other covenant is a complication in itself. Second, the present law is both statutory and non-statutory. Originally the court used its inherent equitable jurisdiction to grant relief from forfeiture. Since those early days there have been major statutory incursions into the law of forfeiture, with the result that there is some uncertainty as to the extent to which the inherent equitable jurisdiction has survived these legislative developments (*Abbey National Building Society* v *Maybeech Ltd* (4) and *Official Custodian for Charities* v *Parway Estates Developments Ltd* (5)). Third, there are different schemes for relief in relation to non-payment of rent between the High Court and county court, which is difficult to justify. Fourth, under the present regime a landlord has to guess accurately whether a given breach is remediable, and also decide how much time to give a tenant to remedy the breach before serving a writ. Finally, waiver is technical and operates irrespective of the merits of the case.

In 1985 the Law Commission published its Report on Forfeitire of Tenancies (6). It recommended that the current law of forfeiture, both statutory and non-statutory, should be abolished and with it the doctrine of re-entry. It was proposed that a landlord should have the right to bring termination order proceedings which would not depend on any clause in the lease (ie no need for a right of re-entry). Such a right could be expressly excluded. Under the new scheme there would be no distinction between termination for non-payment of rent and termination for other reasons. In termination order proceedings the landlord would have to establish a 'termination order event' in order to be successful. These would be: (i) a breach of covenant by the tenant; or (ii) a disguised breach of covenant (broadly a breach by the tenant of an obligation imposed on him otherwise than by covenant); or (iii) the tenant's insolvency. A successful application by a landlord for a termination order would result in either an 'absolute order' (to terminate the tenancy unconditionally on a date specified), or a 'remedial order' (to terminate the tenancy on a date specified unless the tenant has remedied the breach of covenant in conformity with the order of the court by that time). In both cases, the court would have a discretion to grant or refuse to grant an order in accordance with certain guidelines.

In 1994, the Law Commission published a further report which is, in reality, a republication of the 1985 Report with some small changes (7). The latest report includes a draft Termination of Tenancies Bill.

The enactment of the Law Commission's proposals would be advantageous in many respects and would remove much of the current complexity and confusion surrounding this particular area of the law. In particular, bringing to an end the separate procedures for termination for non-payment of rent and termination for other reasons would be a major advance.

References

(1) (1886) 3 TLR 34
(2) [1973] 3 All ER 308
(3) Law Com No 142, 21 March 1985, at para 3.2
(4) [1984] 3 All ER 262
(5) [1984] 3 All ER 679
(6) Law Com No 142
(7) Termination of Tenancies Bill (Law Com No 221)

QUESTION 2

General Comment

An interesting question on licences which gives students a good opportunity to display their knowledge of this area of law. However, the facts of the question are such that the possibility of there being a constructive trust in respect of the bungalow ought to be considered.

Skeleton Solution

Definition of a licence.

Types of licences.

Contractual licence.

Estoppel licence – *Greasley* v *Cooke*.

Enforcement of contractual and estoppel licences against third parties – *Ashburn Anstalt* v *Arnold*.

Constructive trusts – no formalities for creation required – *Binions* v *Evans*.

Suggested Solution

This question is primarily concerned with licences. A licence is a permission given by the occupier of land which allows the licensee to do some act which would otherwise be a trespass. There are four main types of licence. First, there is the bare licence (mere personal permission to be on the licensor's land). Second, a licence may be coupled with the grant of an interest in land, for example a right to enter another man's land to hunt and take away the deer killed. Third, there is the contractual licence (a licence supported by consideration). Finally, there is the estoppel licence. In the context of this question, contractual and estoppel licences are particularly relevant.

In 1988, Jack allows his niece Frances to use his country cottage in the following terms: 'it needs quite a lot doing to it to make it habitable, but you don't need to pay me any rent'. Clearly, Frances does not have a lease. The fact that she is not paying rent does not preclude her from having a lease (*Ashburn Anstalt* v *Arnold &*

Another (1)). The reason she does not have a lease is because her occupancy is for an indefinite period of time, and it is a requirement of a valid lease that it must be of certain duration in the sense that its ultimate date of expiry must be ascertainable at or before the commencement of the term (*Lace* v *Chantler* (2)).

The issue here is what type of licence Frances has. She has more than a bare licence, as by making the cottage habitable and embarking on a poultry business (presumably at the cottage) this implies work and probably expenditure on the cottage by Frances and her boyfriend. Accordingly, it would seem that Frances and her boyfriend have got either a contractual licence or an estoppel licence.

A contractual licence is one granted for valuable consideration (ie Frances has to show that she has given value for it). On the facts it is submitted that the case for a contractual licence is a bit thin. It is necessary to show that Frances has provided value, and she is not paying rent. All she has got to rely upon in this regard is the work done to make the cottage habitable. Even if she could establish a contractual licence it may not avail her much against Paul as the consensus view now is that a contractual licence is not binding on a successor-in-title of the licensor.

On the facts, Frances may have a stronger claim to an estoppel licence. Such a licence arises where A, the owner of land, allows B to spend money on that land or otherwise to act to his detriment under an expectation created or encouraged by A that he will be allowed to remain on the land or acquire an interest in the land. In such circumstances A will not be allowed to defeat that expectation and deny B's right to remain or to an interest in the land (*Ramsden* v *Dyson* (3)). In essence the requirements for an estoppel licence are representation, reliance and detriment. In this case, Frances told Jack about the plan to raise poultry. He in turn offered her the use of his country cottage and indicated that quite a lot needed to be done to render it habitable. Frances and her boyfriend moved into the cottage, made it habitable and set up a poultry business. For an estoppel licence, the prospective licensee must have acted to his detriment (the expenditure of money is the usual evidence of detriment relied upon). Here, Frances and her boyfriend have clearly acted to their detriment by rendering the cottage habitable and establishing the poultry business. It is not unreasonable in the circumstances to infer that Jack knew that they were so acting, and that in the light of his advance knowledge of Frances' plans he had encouraged them to so act. Accordingly, it is submitted that Frances may have an estoppel licence in respect of the cottage (the position of a third party vis-à-vis such a licence is considered below).

Turning to Grace, in 1989 she lost her job and Jack suggested that she should go to live with him in his London home and help him as an unpaid housekeeper and secretary. Such facts are supportive of a contractual licence. A contractual licence is basically an ordinary contract which creates a licence supported by consideration. It creates a contractual right to do things on land which would otherwise be a trespass. Here it could be argued that the contract is that Grace can live in Jack's London house in return for working unpaid as his housekeeper and secretary (ie she is providing consideration).

Further, Grace may be able to establish an estoppel licence if she can prove that Jack allowed her to spend money or alter her position in any way to her detriment in the expectation that she would enjoy some interest in the land. If that is the case, then Jack will be prevented from acting inconsistently with the expectation as raised. Two issues merit consideration in this regard. First, has Jack given Grace an assurance appropriate for an estoppel licence? Second, can Grace show that she has acted to her detriment? The question is not conclusive as to whether, between 1989 and 1992, Jack gave Grace an appropriate assurance. However, in 1992 when he was ill, he told her not to worry about the future since he was going to leave his London house to her in his will. At least since 1992, Grace could show an assurance appropriate for an estoppel licence. There must be detriment for an estoppel licence. However, the fact that Grace has not spent money does not prevent her showing detrimental reliance upon Jack's assurance. In *Greasley* v *Cooke* (4) it was held that the expenditure of money was not a necessary element of detriment. It was sufficient that the party to whom the assurance was given acted on the faith of it in circumstances in which it would be unjust and inequitable for the party making the assurance to go back on it. Accordingly, it is submitted that Grace may have an estoppel licence in respect of the house.

In 1994, Jack died leaving his entire estate to his son Paul. Two issues now have to be addressed. First, can Paul obtain possession of the country cottage from Frances? Second, can he obtain possession of the bungalow from Grace?

As to the country cottage, if, as previously suggested, Frances has an estoppel licence then it is capable of binding a third party (ie Paul). Whether, in practice, Paul would be bound turns on a number of factors. If the land is unregistered, Paul would be bound if he has notice of Frances' interest, because a licence by estoppel is not registerable as a land charge under the Land Charges Act (LCA) 1972 (*ER Ives Investments Ltd* v *High* (5)). If the land is registered Paul will be bound if the estoppel licence has been protected by the entry of a notice or caution on the register, unless it is an overriding interest under s70(1)(g) Land Registration Act (LRA) 1925, in which case he is bound because it *is* an overriding interest (given that Frances is in actual occupation of the cottage she may be able to establish an overriding interest under s70(1)(g)). If Frances has an estoppel licence what remedy will the court grant her to give effect to it? In this regard the courts have shown great flexibility. In *Pascoe* v *Turner* (6) the Court of Appeal held that the licensee's equitable rights arising under the estoppel could only be satisfied by granting to her the fee simple of the house in question. In *Inwards* v *Baker* (7) the licensee was granted a life interest. However, in *Dodsworth* v *Dodsworth* (8) the licensees were only allowed to remain in the property until their expenditure was reimbursed. Unfortunately, such flexibility has produced uncertainty because it is difficult for practitioners to anticipate how the estoppel will be satisfied in a given case. Accordingly, it is a matter of speculation as to what relief Frances would be granted here. What is likely to be crucial to the remedy that Frances is granted is the nature of the assurance given to her by Jack. For example, where there is an assurance that the licensee can remain in the property for as long as he or she wishes, then the court usually so orders. Accordingly, it is crucial for Frances to produce as much relevant evidence as possible as to any assurances given to her by Jack.

Finally, what is the position of Grace in relation to the bungalow? It was suggested above that Grace might have had a contractual licence, or an estoppel licence, in respect of Jack's London house. However, in 1994 Jack sold that house and bought the bungalow and moved to it with Grace who has presumably remained there since his death. It is submitted that these property dealings of Jack before his death will not jeopardise Grace's position because in *Re Basham* (9) it was said that the belief/assurance encouraged in the licensee by the licensor did not have to relate to a particular property. If Grace is deemed to have a contractual licence the current view is that such a licence is not binding on a third party (*Ashburn Anstalt* v *Arnold*). However, as previously noted, an estoppel licence can bind a third party.

Given the clear assurance made by Jack to Grace the court may well find a constructive trust (ie that Paul is holding the legal title to the bungalow on a constructive trust for Grace). A constructive trust arises by operation of law when the court is of the view that it is in the interests of justice that such a trust should be imposed. The courts have frequently protected a licence (both contractual and estoppel) by way of imposing a constructive trust on a purchaser or successor-in-title of the licensor with notice of the licence. Here, it is submitted that Paul is likely to have notice of Grace's licence. Such a use for the constructive trust was first developed by Lord Denning MR in his dissenting judgment in *Binions* v *Evans* (10). Currently, the use of the constructive trust is much favoured by the courts (see Fox LJ in *Ashburn Anstalt* v *Arnold*). The use of the constructive trust in this regard is facilitated by s53(2) Law of Property Act (LPA) 1925 which exempts it from the requirements of s53(1) LPA 1925 (for example, a declaration of trust respecting land must be evidenced by writing signed by some person able to declare the trust or by his will), ie it can arise from a mere oral declaration – like that of Jack to Grace. Accordingly, it is submitted that Grace would have a good case in resisting Paul's claim to possession of the bungalow.

References

(1) [1988] 2 WLR 706
(2) [1944] KB 368
(3) (1865) LR 1 HL 129
(4) [1980] 3 All ER 710
(5) [1967] 2 QB 379
(6) [1979] 1 WLR 431
(7) [1965] 2 QB 29
(8) (1973) 228 EG 1115
(9) [1986] 1 WLR 1498
(10) [1972] Ch 359 – ~~365~~ 591

QUESTION 3

General Comment

The question is primarily concerned with a number of issues relevant to the law of easements. Further, some comment upon estoppel licences would also be appropriate. The question provides students well-versed in these areas of law with a fairly straightforward opportunity to display their knowledge and understanding.

Skeleton Solution

Characteristics of an easement.

Easement of storage.

Acquisition of an easement – express grant, prescription, doctrine of proprietary estoppel.

Registration requirements.

Estoppel licences.

Remedies to give effect to an estoppel licence.

Suggested Solution

An easement is a right in or over the land of another. In order to be an easement the right in question must satisfy the following five characteristics (see *Re Ellenborough Park* (1)): (i) there must be a dominant and servient tenement; (ii) the easement must accommodate the dominant tenement; (iii) the dominant and servient tenements must not be both owned and occupied by the same person; (iv) a right over land cannot amount to an easement unless it is capable of forming the subject matter of a grant; and (v) the right must be against other land (ie it is not a right to possession of other land).

Here, Bob is storing building materials in Frank's old shed. The first four characteristics of an easement listed above would appear to be satisfied. For example, there is a dominant tenement (Bob's adjoining land) and a servient tenement (Frank's land). However, there might be a problem with the final characteristic – an easement cannot be a right to possession of other land (ie the right claimed must not amount to joint use of the servient tenement by the dominant owner). In essence the issue is: can there be an easement of storage? Case law on this point is somewhat conflicting. In *Copeland* v *Greenhalf* (2) a claim to stand an unlimited number of vehicles on another's land was held not to be capable of being an easement because it was held to amount to a claim to joint possession of the land (orthodox line taken). However, in *Wright* v *Macadam* (3) the Court of Appeal upheld the right of a tenant to store her coal in a shed on the landlord's land. Further, in *Attorney-General of Southern Nigeria* v *John Holt & Co (Liverpool) Ltd* (4) the courts recognised as an easement the right to store casks and trade-produce on land. The decision in *Wright* v *Macadam*, in particular, has been the subject of much comment and criticism. Accordingly, given the current state of authority there must be some doubt as to whether the right being claimed by Bob can exist as an easement. However, for the purposes of this question let us assume that it can.

In order for a right to be an easement, not only must it satisfy the characteristics of an easement, it must be properly acquired as an easement. There are a variety of ways in which an easement can be acquired. In the context of this question three methods of acquisition deserve comment – express grant, prescription under the Prescription Act 1832 and estoppel.

Here, Frank, in response to Bob's request to store building materials on Frank's land, said: 'Of course. You can use that old shed adjoining your land.' An express grant of an easement is usually made by the use of express words in the conveyance of the legal estate of the dominant tenement, and provided it is granted for a period of time equivalent to a freehold or leasehold estate, and the conveyance itself complies with the formal requirements (ie it is made by deed), the easement will be legal. Here, there is an oral grant. It has been held that an oral grant can succeed as an equitable easement when supported by an act of part-performance (*McManus* v *Cooke* (5) and *May* v *Belville* (6)). Bob's use of the shed would rank as an act of part-performance. Accordingly, it is submitted that Bob could have acquired the easement by express grant. However, both the aforementioned decisions pre-dated the coming into force of s2 Law of Property (Miscellaneous Provisions) Act 1989, in consequence of which this method of acquisition (oral grant supported by an act of part performance) may no longer be available.

The basis of holding that an easement is acquired by prescription is that if long user as of right is proved the courts will presume that the use began lawfully, ie as a result of a grant.

The basis of holding that an easement is acquired by prescription is that if long user as of right is proved the courts will presume that the use began lawfully, ie as a result of a grant. Since Bob's user commenced 25 years ago, in 1970, it is necessary to consider the possibility of him having acquired an easement by prescription. One of the prerequisites of prescription is user as of right, ie the use must have been exercised without force, without secrecy and, most significantly for the purposes of this question, without permission. Of the three methods of acquiring an easement by prescription the one which may be of most assistance to Bob is the Prescription Act 1832. In order to establish a claim under the Act to an easement other than light, Bob must show user as of right, user without interruption and user for one of the statutory periods (shorter period is 20 years, longer period is 40 years). Under the Act, user as of right has the same meaning as above, except that there are specific rules relating to the effect of permission. Such rules are particularly relevant here since Frank gave Bob oral permission to store material in the old shed. Under the 1832 Act, an oral consent given at the outset of user (and extending throughout) defeats a claim under the shorter period but not the longer period. Here, since user commenced in 1970, it is not feasible to utilise the longer period. As to the shorter period, since Frank gave Bob oral permission at the outset this would seem to preclude any possibility of successfully establishing a claim under the 20-year period of the Act (*Healey* v *Hawkins* (7)). Further, to acquire an easement under the Act it is necessary to litigate because s4 provides that both the 20 and 40-year periods must be 'next before action', ie both periods are measured backwards from the action in which the right is questioned.

Finally, in relation to acquisition of an easement it may be possible for Bob to argue that he has acquired an easement by operation of the doctrine of proprietary estoppel. This method of acquisition covers a situation where no formal grant of an easement is made but an easement arises in consequence of the conduct of the parties. For example, in *Crabb* v *Arun District Council* (8) Crabb owned two plots of land only one of which (Plot A) had an exit to the highway. The local authority led Crabb to believe that he would be allowed a right of way across their land onto the highway from Plot B if he sold Plot A. In reliance upon this assurance, Crabb sold Plot A without reserving a right of way across it from Plot B to the exit. There was no formal grant of an easement by the local authority. Shortly afterwards the local authority fenced off the exit point from Plot B which they had installed. Crabb sought an injunction. The Court of Appeal concluded that the local authority were estopped from going back on their assurance and they granted Crabb a right of way across the council's land, free of charge. Here, if Bob can show that Frank or Gus gave him an assurance as to his use of the shed prior to the reroofing, then the reroofing could be used as detrimental reliance upon the assurance and thus establish the estoppel. An easement created by estoppel can only be equitable.

Accordingly, as to acquisition, it is submitted that Bob may have acquired an easement either by an oral express grant or by estoppel. In either case, the easement would rank as an equitable one (for an easement to be legal it must be created by deed and be granted for a period of time equivalent to a freehold or leasehold estate). The enforcement of an equitable easement against a purchaser of the servient land (ie Spike) turns on several factors, including whether the land is registered or unregistered. In the case of unregistered land an equitable easement must be registered as a Class D(iii) land charge to bind a purchaser for value. Accordingly, if so registered, Spike would be bound by it. However, if not registered as a land charge Spike might still be bound if he knew about Bob's use of the shed (*ER Ives Investments Ltd* v *High* (9)). In the case of registered land the equitable easement is an overriding interest by virtue of *Celsteel Ltd* v *Alton House Holdings Ltd* (10), and thus binding on Spike.

Given that there is some uncertainty as to whether the right Bob is claiming is capable of existing as an easement, it is worth considering whether any possibilities other than easements are open to him.

In the circumstances it may be possible for Bob to argue that he has an estoppel licence. It has long been accepted that a licensor is estopped from revoking a licence where he has acquiesced to or encouraged the use of land. Bob might be able to show that Frank or Gus have so acted – Gus never objected to Bob's use of the shed. Further, and very importantly here, given that Gus has sold the land on which the shed is located to Spike, an estoppel licence can bind a third party. Whether in practice Spike would be bound turns on a number of factors. If the land is unregistered, Spike would be bound if he has notice of Bob's right because a licence by estoppel is not registerable as a land charge under the Land Charges Act 1972 (*ER Ives Investments Ltd* v *High*). If the land is registered Spike would be bound if the estoppel licence has been protected by the entry of a notice or caution on the register, unless it is an overriding interest under s70(1)(g) LRA 1925, which in this case it is not.

Finally, if the court found that Bob had an estoppel licence what remedy would they grant to give effect to it (ie satisfy the equity)?

In this regard the courts have shown great flexibility (ranging from a transfer of the fee simple to the licensee to reasonable notice to quit). Such flexibility has produced uncertainty because it is difficult for practitioners to anticipate how the estoppel will be applied in a given situation. Here it is submitted that Bob would get reasonable notice to quit the shed and reimbursement of any monies spent by him in reroofing it.

References

(1) [1956] Ch 131
(2) [1952] Ch 488
(3) [1949] 2 KB 744
(4) [1915] AC 599
(5) (1887) 35 Ch D 681
(6) [1905] 2 Ch 605
(7) [1968] 1 WLR 1967
(8) [1976] Ch 179
(9) [1967] 2 QB 379
(10) [1985] 1 WLR 204

QUESTION 4

General Comment

A fairly straightforward essay title on a mainstream area of mortgages which would give students well-versed in the relevant law a good opportunity to exhibit their knowledge and understanding. Essential to have a good grasp of the relevant case law.

Skeleton Solution

Definition of a mortgage.

No clogs or fetters on the equity of redemption.

Definition of a collateral advantage.

Initial attitude of the courts.

Role of equity.

Three classes of collateral advantage – those that are: (1) unconscionable and oppressive (*Cityland and Property (Holdings) Ltd* v *Dabrah*); (2) enforceable for the duration of the mortgage (*Biggs* v *Hoddinott*); and (3) capable of surviving redemption of the mortgage (*Kreglinger* v *New Patagonia Meat & Cold Storage Co Ltd*).

Suggested Solution

A mortgage is essentially a transaction whereby an interest in property, be it land, house or business, is transferred to a mortgagee (lender) as security for the loan subject to a right of redemption vested in the mortgagor (borrower).

Once a mortgage is entered into the equity of redemption comes into existence – this is the borrower's right of ownership of the property subject to the mortgage. Equity protects the borrower's equity of redemption through the maxim 'once a mortgage always a mortgage'. One of the ways in which this maxim is applied is that there must be no clog or fetter on the equity of redemption. This means that the borrower cannot be stopped from (a) ultimately redeeming his property, and (b) redeeming it free from any condition in the mortgage.

The basic purpose of a mortgage is to provide security for the repayment of the money lent by the mortgagee. However, in the case of commercial properties the lender may succeed in negotiating for some additional advantage (collateral advantages are not usually encountered in mortgages of domestic properties). For example, a brewery will often advance money on mortgage to the licensee of a public house, provided the borrower agrees to buy all his beer from the lending brewery. Comparable arrangements are often made between petrol companies and garage owners.

The original view of the courts was that all collateral advantages taken by a lender were void. This was because they were regarded as a disguised form of interest, contravening the old usury laws (*Jennings* v *Ward* (1)). In 1854 the last of the statutes dealing with usury was repealed and thereafter the attitude of the courts to collateral advantages began to change.

The quotation given in the question comes from the judgment of Lord Parker in *Kreglinger* v *New Patagonia Meat and Cold Storage Co Ltd* (2). It is true to say that today there is no rule of equity which prevents a lender from stipulating for a collateral advantage. Rather, equity endeavours to 'hold the ring' so far as collateral advantages are concerned.

Equity divides collateral advantages into three classes. First, the collateral advantage may be held to be unconscionable and oppressive if it was imposed in a morally reprehensive way. In such a case the collateral advantage is void and therefore unenforceable even during the currency of the mortgage. In *Cityland & Property Holdings Ltd* v *Dabrah* (3) a term in the mortgage which imposed an extremely high premium, rather than requiring payment of interest, was held to be unenforceable as being oppressive and unreasonable because the whole balance of the premium and loan became immediately repayable on default. The mortgage was rewritten by the court.

Second, the collateral advantage may be regarded as fair and enforceable for the duration of the mortgage (many solus ties come within this second class). In *Biggs* v *Hoddinott* (4) a mortgage of a public house was granted by a brewer to a publican. The mortgage required the borrower to take all his beer from the mortgagee during the currency of the mortgage (ie a solus agreement).

The Court of Appeal upheld the collateral advantage as valid. Chitty LJ put the matter thus:

> 'The present appears to me to be a reasonable trade bargain between two businessmen who enter into it with their eyes open and it would be a fanciful doctrine of equity that would set it aside' (5).

So far as solus agreements are concerned, they come within the category of agreements in restraint of trade and must therefore be justified on the ground of reasonableness (*Esso Petroleum Co Ltd* v *Harper's Garage (Stourport) Ltd* (6)). Accordingly, in such cases, the test is unreasonableness not unconscionability. Equity will intervene if the solus agreement is unreasonable, ie an excessive restraint of trade.

Third, the collateral advantage may survive redemption of the mortgage. Normally a collateral advantage will not survive redemption of the mortgage (even if the mortgagor has agreed to a term that the collateral advantage shall continue beyond redemption), for otherwise the borrower would get back an estate encumbered in a way that the estate he mortgaged was not. Nevertheless, in the case of commercial mortgages entered into by parties bargaining on equal terms, the courts may be prepared to enforce a collateral advantage even after redemption by treating it as if it was a separate agreement, part of the consideration for entering the mortgage. The lead case in this regard is *Kreglinger* v *New Patagonia Meat Co Ltd*. There, a meat company mortgaged its property to a wool-broker. It was a term of the mortgage that the mortgagor would for five years offer its sheepskins to the mortgagee for purchase. Although the mortgage was redeemed after two years the House of Lords held that the option was valid even though it continued for three years after redemption. The option was regarded as being reasonable – it was for a short period of time and the mortgagee had to pay the best price for the sheepskins. The collateral advantage here was seen as forming part of a bigger commercial deal done between the two parties well capable of looking after their own interests (ie it was a separate agreement, not really part of the mortgage).

Finally, it is true that there is now no rule of equity which prevents a mortgagee from stipulating for a collateral advantage. However, in certain circumstances, the courts will still be prepared to strike down a collateral advantage. The present position can be summarised as follows: a collateral advantage which exists until redemption can be valid, but will be struck down if it is oppressive or unconscionable; a collateral advantage which exists beyond redemption will be struck down unless it exists as an independent transaction.

References

(1) (1705) 2 Vern 520
(2) [1914] AC 25

References (continued)

(3) [1968] Ch 166
(4) [1898] 2 Ch 307
(5) Ibid at p322
(6) [1968] AC 269

QUESTION 5

General Comment

This question is primarily concerned with the enforcement of freehold covenants against successors-in-title of the original parties. In addition, some coverage of the enforcement of leasehold covenants is required (such a question structure was doubtless designed to test whether students were aware of the different enforcement regimes between the two types of covenant). As with most problem questions on this topic, the inclusion of a diagrammatical representation of the facts is advisable, not least because it should eliminate the possibility of a student confusing the various parties in the course of an answer.

Skeleton Solution

Freehold covenants

Definition of a covenant.

Distinguishing between positive and restrictive covenants.

Indirect devices for enforcement of positive covenants.

Running of the burden of a restrictive covenant in equity.

Running of the benefit of a restrictive covenant in equity – express annexation, statutory annexation (*Federated Homes Ltd* v *Mill Lodge Properties Ltd*) and schemes of development.

Registration.

Leasehold covenants

Formalities for creation of a legal lease.

Assignment of a lease.

Privity of estate.

Suggested Solution

Freehold covenants

A covenant in the context of real property law is an agreement by deed whereby one party (the covenantor) promises with another party (the covenantee) that he will or will not engage in some stated activity in relation to a specified piece of land. The land owned by the covenantee will have the benefit of the covenant and that owned by the covenantor will have the burden. Here, on the sale of Plot A to Vince there are two sets of covenants. First, Vince (original covenator) entered into covenants for the benefit of Alfred (original covenantee) and his successors. Second, Alfred (original covenantor) entered into covenants for the benefit of Vince (original covenantee) and his successors.

There are two kinds of freehold covenant – positive and restrictive. A positive covenant is one which obliges the owner to do something on his land (a work covenant, eg a covenant to fence) or to contribute money towards work to be done or services to be provided for the benefit of his land (a money covenant, eg a covenant to contribute towards the construction or maintenance of a private road). A restrictive covenant is one which restrains a landowner in some respect from the uninhibited use of his property, eg a covenant which prevents the covenantor from using his land for the purpose of conducting trade and business. Here, Vince's covenant to maintain the garden of Plot A and the dividing wall in good condition, and Alfred's covenant to maintain the garden on Plot B in good condition are positive ones, while the covenants to use the houses on Plots A and B for residential purposes only are restrictive ones.

The factual developments recounted in the question can be represented diagrammatically as follows:

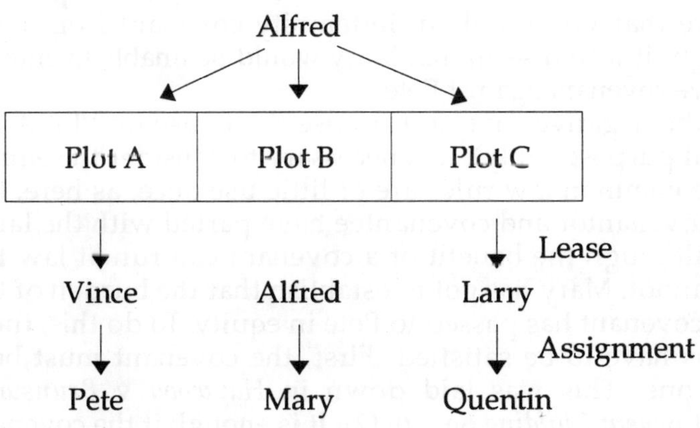

Mary, Alfred's successor-in-title in respect of Plot B, wishes to know whether she can enforce the covenants originally entered into by Vince on purchasing Plot A from Alfred against Pete, and whether she can enforce the covenants originally entered into by Larry on the leasing of Plot C against Quentin. The issues in respect of Plot A will be dealt with first and those in respect of Plot C second.

For Mary to be able to enforce the covenant to use the house on Plot A for residential purposes only and the covenant to maintain the garden and dividing wall in good condition against Pete she has to show that the burden of these covenants has passed to him, and that the benefit of them has passed to her under either the common law or equity rules.

Dealing first with the positive covenant (to maintain the garden and dividing wall in good condition), the burden of such a convenant cannot run directly with freehold land either at law or in equity (*Austerberry* v *Corporation of Oldham* (1)). However, certain indirect devices (none of which are fool-proof) are resorted to by conveyancers to try to circumvent the latter rule. In the circumstances, the indirect device which could be of assistance is the chain of indemnity covenants. For this device to be available it would have been necessary for Vince to have taken a covenant of indemnity from Pete when he sold Plot A to him. Vince should have so acted because as an original covenantor he remains liable on the covenant on the basis of privity of contract even after he has parted with the land. (If there was such a covenant, once Vince was sued he would then sue Pete on the indemnity covenant – in practice both actions would be consolidated.) It is only through such an indirect device that the positive covenant will be enforceable against Pete. However, there is nothing in the question to indicate that Vince took an indemnity covenant from Pete. Accordingly, it would seem that Mary would be unable to enforce the positive covenant against Pete.

As to the negative covenant (to use the house on Plot A for residential purposes only), it is necessary to consider the equity rules. The common law rules are of little use once, as here, the original covenantor and covenantee have parted with the land, because although the benefit of a covenant can run at law the burden cannot. Mary has got to establish that the burden of the negative covenant has passed to Pete in equity. To do this, three conditions have to be satisfied. First, the covenant must be a negative one. This was laid down in *Haywood* v *Brunswick Permanent Benefit Building Society* (2). It is enough if the covenant is negative in nature. Here, the covenant is negative in nature, though worded positively (the house cannot be used for any purposes other than residential ones). Second, the covenant must have been made for the protection of land retained by the covenantee (*London County Council* v *Allen* (3)). Here, it would seem that the covenant was made for the protection of Plot B, retained by

Alfred. Third, the burden of the covenant must have been intended to run with the covenantor's (Vince's) land. By virtue of s79 Law of Property Act (LPA) 1925, covenants relating to the covenantor's land which are made after 1925 are deemed to have been made by the covenantor on behalf of himself, his successors-in-title and the persons deriving title under him or them unless a contrary intention appears. Since here the covenant was entered into after 1925, and there is no such contrary intention, this third requirement would be satisfied. Accordingly, it seems that the burden of the restrictive covenant has passed to Pete.

There is one final matter to consider in relation to the burden of the restrictive covenant – registration. Where, as here, the land is unregistered the restrictive covenant must be registered as a Class D (ii) land charge under the Land Charges Act (LCA) 1972 since it was entered into after 1925. Failure to so register the covenant would render it void against a purchaser for value of a legal estate in the land (s4(6) LCA 1972). For the purposes of this question it is assumed that this registration requirement has been satisfied.

Having shown that the burden of the restrictive covenant can pass to Pete in equity it is now necessary for Mary to show that the benefit of the covenant has passed to her in equity. For the benefit of a restrictive covenant to pass in equity to a successor-in-title of a covenantee the covenant must 'touch and concern' or 'benefit' some land of the covenantee, and the benefit must be transmitted in one or more of the ways prescribed by equity (annexation, assignment or scheme of development). Here the covenant to use the house (on Plot A) for residential purposes only clearly touches and concerns Plot B. The key issue is whether the benefit has passed to Mary in one or more of the ways recognised by equity.

In this regard it is necessary to consider annexation. Express annexation confers the benefit of the covenant upon the land, not individuals. Whether the benefit is so annexed to the land depends upon the wording of the covenants. In particular, it must be possible to identify the land to be benefited from such wording. In *Rogers* v *Hosegood* (4) the covenant was deemed to be annexed since it referred to the dominant land. However, in *Renals* v *Cowlishaw* (5) the covenant was not annexed because it only referred to 'the vendors, their heirs, executors, administrators and assigns' (ie no reference was made to any land). Here the covenant was made 'with Alfred and his successors-in-title'. This may not be enough for express annexation because there is no real identification of the benefited land.

However, statutory annexation is likely to be of help to Mary. In *Federated Homes Ltd* v *Mill Lodge Properties Ltd* (6) the Court of Appeal held that where a restrictive covenant touches and concerns the covenantee's land, s78(1) LPA 1925 annexes the benefit of the covenant to the covenantee's land and the covenant is enforceable at the suit of the covenantee and his successors-in-title. On the strength of *Federated Homes* it would seem that Mary could show that the benefit of the covenant has passed to her. However, it is important to note that while the decision in *Federated Homes* was good news for conveyancers (s78 could come to the rescue if the express annexation formula used by them turned out be deficient), the reasoning of the Court of Appeal on that occasion is not beyond criticism. Accordingly, provided Mary can show statutory annexation (which seems likely) she will be able to enforce the restrictive covenant against Pete.

Further, it may also be possible for Mary to show that the land is subject to a scheme of development, given that in 1980 Alfred divided a piece of undeveloped land into three plots. The requirements for a scheme of development were first laid down in *Elliston* v *Reacher* (7). Today, it seems that for such a scheme to exist two requirements have to be satisfied. First, the area of the scheme must be defined. Second, those who purchase from the creator of the scheme do so on the footing that all purchasers should be mutually bound by and mutually entitled to enforce a defined set of restrictions. Clearly, if a scheme of development can be established it could be pleaded by Mary, together with statutory annexation.

Leasehold covenants

Finally, can Mary enforce against Quentin the covenants originally entered into by Larry when he took the 99-year lease of Plot C from Alfred? Given that it is for more than three years it is crucial that the lease was made by deed in order to create a legal estate: s52(1) LPA 1925. Further, a legal lease, once created, can only be transferred inter vivos by deed: s52 LPA 1925. For the purposes of this answer it is assumed that the relevant formalities have been complied with, both in respect of the creation of the lease between Alfred and Larry and its assignment by Larry to Quentin. The reason why it is crucial to ascertain if we are dealing with a legal lease here is because if we are then privity of estate exists. The enforcement of a leasehold covenant between assignees either of the lease (ie Quentin) or of the reversion, depends upon whether there is privity of estate between plaintiff and defendant, and whether the covenant in question touches and concerns the land

(*Spencer's Case* (8)). Here the covenants to use the house on Plot C for residential purposes only and to maintain the garden and dividing wall in good condition clearly touch and concern the land. If privity of estate can be established then all covenants, whether positive or negative, are enforceable. If Mary can show that there is privity of estate between herself and Quentin then she would be able to enforce the covenants against him. Mary could show that there is privity of estate between herself and Quentin by establishing that she acquired the freehold reversion of Plot C from Alfred. However, there is no suggestion in the question that she has so acted. Accordingly, it would seem that Mary cannot enforce the covenants against Quentin.

References

(1) (1885) 29 Ch D 750
(2) (1881) 8 QBD 403
(3) [1914] 3 KB 642
(4) [1900] 2 Ch 388 623
(5) (1879) 11 Ch D 866
(6) [1980] 1 WLR 594
(7) [1908] 2 Ch 374 631
(8) (1583) 5 Co Rep 16

Elliston v. Reacher

The conditions for scheme of developments.

1. both the plaintiff & defendant must have purchased their land from a common vendor.

2. Before sale the vendor has laid out his land in plots and all restrictions were intended and were common for all plots.

3- The restrictions are for the benefit and advancement of plots of land.

QUESTION 6

General Comment

This is a question primarily concerned with co-ownership. However, it is not a straightforward co-ownership question because it contains an additional dimension (Brenda). In terms of structuring an answer, it is probably better to look at the co-ownership issues first and then consider the position of Brenda.

Skeleton Solution

Co-ownership trust for sale – ss34–36 LPA 1925.

Legal title on a joint tenancy.

Beneficial interest on a joint tenancy.

Principle of survivorship.

Severance of beneficial interest: *Burgess* v *Rawnsley*.

Section 30 LPA 1925 – application for order of sale – secondary trust: *Jones* v *Challenger*.

Resulting trusts: *Dyer* v *Dyer*; *Bull* v *Bull*.

Presumption of advancement.

Suggested Solution

The question requires consideration of a number of issues concerning co-ownership. However, the situation is somewhat complicated by the position of Brenda in relation to the house. In the ensuing paragraphs the co-ownership issues are considered first and then the position of Brenda is evaluated. Further, the question requires not only a general discussion of the issues involved, but also consideration of how the proceeds would be distributed in the eventuality of the house being sold.

A trust for sale arises where there are concurrent interests in land (ie where more than one person holds interests in the land at the same time). Accordingly, the persons holding the interests are co-owners. Today, for all practical purposes, there are two types of co-ownership – joint tenancy and tenancy in common. In cases of co-ownership it is vital to distinguish between ownership at law and ownership in equity (ie beneficial ownership). Since 1 January

1926, the legal estate in the case of co-owned land must be held on a joint tenancy: s1 Law of Property Act (LPA) 1925.

Here Brenda bought a large house for her three daughters and agreed for the house to be conveyed into the names of her three daughters as 'beneficial joint tenants'. Accordingly, there are concurrent interests in land (ie co-ownership) and the legal estate is held on a joint tenancy by Iris, Jill and Kirsten.

Although the legal estate in co-owned land must always be held on a joint tenancy, the equitable interest can be held on either a joint tenancy or a tenancy in common. In determining how the equitable interest is held, the general rule is that a grant to two or more persons without words of severance (words in the grant which show that the tenants are each to take a distinct share in the property, eg 'share and share alike') creates a beneficial joint tenancy. To this general rule there are two qualifications. First, there are certain circumstances in which equity may presume that a tenancy in common was intended, unless there is an express indication to the contrary. Second, a joint tenancy cannot exist without the presence of the four unities (time, title, interest and possession). On the facts, there are no words of severance here. Further, there is nothing in the question to suggest that either qualification to the general rule is applicable here. Accordingly, it is submitted that Iris, Jill and Kirsten are holding the legal title on trust for sale for themselves as beneficial joint tenants in equity (ie the beneficial interest is held on a joint tenancy). The aforementioned conclusions about the legal estate and equitable interest can be represented diagrammatically as follows:

Legal Estate	Equitable Interest
I + J + K	I + J + K
Joint Tenancy	Joint Tenancy

One of the hallmarks of a joint tenancy is the principle of survivorship. On the death of one joint tenant his interest in the land passes to the other joint tenants by the right of survivorship. This right takes precedence over any disposition made in a joint tenant's will.

It is possible to sever the equitable joint tenancy without

disturbing the joint tenancy of the legal estate. However, in view of the principle of survivorship such severance must be done during the joint tenant's lifetime. Severance is clearly relevant here. Iris has married and moved out of the house. Jill and Kirsten agree to buy her beneficial interest in the house, but before this can be effected Iris is killed in a car accident. The issue here is whether or not Iris severed her beneficial interest in the house before her death. In *Burgess* v *Rawnsley* (1) the Court of Appeal unanimously held that an oral agreement between two joint tenants for one to buy the other's share was sufficient to evince an intention by them that the beneficial joint tenancy ought to be severed, even though the agreement was unenforceable because of non-compliance with s40 LPA 1925. (The significance of the agreement was not that it bound the parties, but that it served as an indication of a common intention to sever.) It was a course of dealing which was sufficient to effect a severance. On the strength of this case it could be argued that here the joint tenants had evinced an intention to sever. Iris had moved out and Jill and Kirsten agreed to buy her interest in the house. Here, since the agreement between the joint tenants was not 'made in writing' to satisfy s2 of the Law of Property (Miscellaneous Provisions) Act 1989 (which repealed s40 LPA 1925), the agreement between Iris, Jill and Kirsten is unenforceable. However, an intention to sever could be found, in which case Iris' one-third share henceforward would have been held on a tenancy in common, and on her death would have passed under her will or intestacy. On Iris' death the legal title remains in Jill and Kirsten.

Following Jill's posting abroad she suggests that the house should be sold. Brenda is opposed to selling (presumably because she wants to continue living in the 'granny flat' in the basement), and the question gives no indication as to Kirsten's view of the matter. As to Jill's desire to sell the house it is important to remember that as co-owned land is held on trust for sale there is a duty on the trustees (ie Jill and Kirsten) to sell subject to a power to postpone sale if exercised unanimously (*Re Mayo* (2)). By virtue of s30 LPA 1925 the court can 'make such order as it thinks fit' on an application by 'any person interested' in co-owned property. If Kirsten is not prepared to sell then Jill would seek a sale order under s30. However, if the trustees are prepared to sell the house then Brenda could be expected to take action under s30 LPA 1925. Upon an application under s30 LPA 1925 the court will look for any 'secondary' or 'collateral' purpose to the trust – that is any reason for the purchase of the house other than sale. Here there is such a secondary purpose – it was understood by all concerned that Brenda would live in the 'granny flat' in the basement for the rest of her life. Where the court finds the existence of a secondary purpose, and where that purpose is still, as here, subsisting, the court will not usually grant a sale order (*Jones* v *Challenger* (3)). Accordingly, on the facts it is likely that the court will postpone a sale until Brenda dies.

If the house were sold how would the proceeds be divided? It is here that the additional dimension of the question becomes particularly relevant. Brenda provided all the money to buy the house, but agreed to convey it into the names of her three daughters. Where land is conveyed to one person P, but the purchase money is provided by another, A, as purchaser, there is a resulting trust in favour of the person providing the purchase money, ie A (*Dyer* v *Dyer* (4)). Likewise, where, as here, the legal estate is in the name of more than one person but where another – not holding the legal estate nor expressed to be a beneficiary – contributes, a resulting trust could arise (*Bull* v *Bull* (5)). However, these are only presumptions which can be rebutted, either by evidence that P (in the above example) was intended to benefit or by the presumption of advancement. Under the presumption of advancement, where a father or other person in loco parentis transfers property into the name of a child, the transaction does not create a resulting trust for the transferor but is an advancement or gift to the child, unless there is evidence of a contrary intention at the time of the transaction. Here, a mother (Brenda) transferred the property to her daughters. The traditional view is that the presumption of advancement would not apply to such a transfer. The courts currently seem to take the approach articulated by Jessel MR in *Bennett* v *Bennett* (6):

> 'In the case of a mother ... it is easier to prove a gift than in the case of a stranger: in the case of a mother very little evidence beyond the relationship is wanted.'

Thus the courts start from the position of a presumption of a resulting trust in favour of the mother which can be easily rebutted. Accordingly, if Jill and Kirsten can show that when their mother bought the house she intended them and Iris to benefit, then the presumption of resulting trust in favour of Brenda can be rebutted. If the presumption can be so rebutted then on a sale of the house the proceeds, it is submitted, would be divided one-third to those entitled under Iris' will or intestacy, with the remaining two-thirds going to Jill and Kirsten. However, if the presumption of resulting trust is not rebutted it could be the case that Brenda would be deemed to hold the entire beneficial interest in the house.

References

(1) [1975] Ch 429
(2) [1943] Ch 302
(3) [1961] 1 QB 176
(4) (1788) 2 Cox Eq Cas 92
(5) [1955] 1 QB 234
(6) (1879) 10 Ch D 474

QUESTION 7

General Comment

A mixed question which touches upon several areas of land law including matrimonial property, licences, leases and aspects of registration. It provides students well-versed in the relevant areas with a fairly straightforward opportunity to display their knowledge and understanding. Not a question for students who had only revised some of, but not all, the areas covered.

Skeleton Solution

Legal estate in one party.

Acquisition of a beneficial interest – indirect contributions, constructive trusts.

Overriding interest under s70(1)(g) LRA 1925.

Periodic tenancy.

Contractual licence – *Errington* v *Errington*.

Estoppel licence.

Suggested Solution

In view of the fact that Barbara provided all the purchase money for the house, and had it registered in her sole name, it is necessary to see if Janet can establish an interest in the property which will be binding on the building company to whom Barbara subsequently sold the house. Having regard to the facts of the question, it would seem appropriate to consider whether Janet has acquired a beneficial interest, a periodic tenancy or a licence.

A person not on the legal title can acquire a beneficial interest in a variety of ways including by way of resulting or constructive trust. For example, a direct contribution to acquisition of the property (contribution to purchase price or mortgage instalments, paying legal costs, etc) will give rise to a resulting trust with the size of the shares being proportionate to the parties' contributions. Here, since Barbara paid the whole of the purchase price, this rules out any form of direct financial contribution by Janet to the acquisition of the house. While a direct contribution to acquisition is clearly sufficient to acquire a beneficial interest, the position as to indirect contributions is much more difficult. In essence Janet is relying upon indirect contributions, ie 'repairs and other outgoings'. Formerly the courts sometimes took a liberal approach to indirect contributions (*Hazell* v *Hazell* (1)). However, that approach has now been rejected. For example, in *Burns* v *Burns* (2) a woman whose contribution amounted to paying for the housekeeping and some bills, as well as buying some electrical appliances and furniture, was held not to have a beneficial interest. In *Lloyds Bank* v *Rosset* (3) the House of Lords laid down guidelines concerning indirect contributions and constructive trusts (which traditionally has been the mechanism used to give effect to a beneficial interest arising by indirect contributions). Where there is an express oral declaration or agreement between the legal title owner and the other party (which does not meet the requirements of s53 Law of Property Act (LPA) 1925) then for a constructive trust to be imposed the other party has to have relied on the agreement to his/her detriment (ie there has to be common intention and detrimental reliance). Detrimental reliance is shown by significant contributions in money or money's worth which need not be direct (*Grant* v *Edwards* (4)). In *Lloyds Bank* v *Rosset* the claim of Mrs Rosset to a beneficial interest based on her interior decorating and supervision of builders carrying out renovation work was unsuccessful. Lord Bridge said that what Mrs Rosset was relying upon as a contribution, when set against the cost of the property which exceeded £70,000, was 'so trifling as to be almost de minimis'. Here it is submitted that Janet will be unlikely to be able to establish a beneficial interest in the house – the facts are not supportive of any common intention between Barbara, Tim and Janet to share the beneficial interest, nor are contributions to repairs and other outgoings likely to be regarded as significant contributions in money or money's worth for purposes of detrimental reliance.

Since this is registered land, if Janet could establish an equitable interest in the house she might be able to claim an overriding interest under s70(1)(g) Land Registration Act (LRA) 1925. Overriding interests bind a purchaser without appearing on the register and even though he has no knowledge of them. There are three aspects to establishing an overriding interest under s70(1)(g). First, the claimant must have a proprietary interest in the property (eg an equitable interest). Second, the claimant must be in actual occupation of the land prior to completion of the transaction (*Abbey National Building Society* v *Cann* (5)). Whether a person is in actual occupation is a question of fact and degree. There must be some degree of permanence and continuation, not a mere fleeting presence. It is submitted that Janet could show a degree of permanence and continuity as to her occupation, and this would not be destroyed just because she was temporarily absent on holiday at the time Barbara sold the house to the building company. Third, if an enquiry is made by a prospective purchaser and the right is not disclosed (because of active concealment on the part of the person claiming an overriding interest under para (g)), then the purchaser will take free of that right. Here Janet's main problem with claiming an overriding interest under s70(1)(g) LRA 1925, which would be binding on the new registered proprietor, is that, as previously mentioned, she is unlikely to be able to show that she has an equitable interest in the house.

Next, it is necessary to see if Janet has a lease as she is paying a token monthly rent and after the marriage breaks down she continues to do so. A periodic tenancy (from week to week or month to month) can be created, either by express agreement or by inference – such as that arising from the payment and acceptance of rent measured by reference to the period in question (week or month, etc). In this case there is obviously no express agreement as the payments are against Barbara's wishes. Nevertheless, if Barbara accepted these payments from Janet, then it is submitted that Janet could have a monthly periodic tenancy by inference. However, a monthly periodic tenancy is not very advantageous to Janet vis-à-vis the new registered proprietor, since such a tenancy can be brought to an end by the tenant being given a month's notice to quit (subject to any contrary agreement between the parties).

Finally, it is necessary to consider whether Janet has a licence which would be binding on the building company.

A contractual licence is one granted for valuable consideration (ie Janet has to show that she has given value for it. Clearly, Janet could show she has given value because she is paying rent and is responsible for repairs and other outgoings. If Janet has a contractual licence would it bind the building company? Originally, contractual licences were seen as personal transactions between the parties and not creating any interest which would be enforceable against a third party (*Clore* v *Theatrical Properties Ltd* (6)). However, in *Errington* v *Errington and Woods* (7) the Court of Appeal held that a contractual licence was binding on a third party except a purchaser for value without notice. Thereafter there was much uncertainty as to whether a contractual licence could bind a third party or not, with cases going either way. The position was substantially clarified in *Ashburn Anstalt* v *Arnold* (8) when the

Court of Appeal (albeit obiter) held that a contractual licence did not bind a third party and that *Errington* v *Errington and Woods* had been wrongly decided on this point. Accordingly, establishing that Janet has a contractual licence will not avail her much since it is not likely to be binding on the building company.

The other possibility for Janet in respect of licences is to try to show that she has an estoppel licence. Such a licence arises as follows. If a landowner (Barbara) allows another person (Janet) to spend money or alter his position to his detriment in the expectation that he will enjoy some privilege or interest in the land, then the owner will be prevented (ie estopped) from acting inconsistently with that expectation. In essence the requirements of an estoppel licence are representation, reliance and detriment. The main attraction for Janet in establishing an estoppel licence is that such a licence is capable of binding a third party (ie the building company). The possible problem for Janet in this regard is showing that Barbara made an appropriate representation, or created an expectation in Janet vis-à-vis the house, since the facts given are not really conclusive of this matter. Janet can certainly show expenditure of money on the house, and the expenditure of money is the usual evidence of detriment relied upon in such cases. Further, since this is registered land, for a third party to be bound by the estoppel licence it has to be protected by the entry of a notice or caution on the register, unless it is an overriding interest under s70(1)(g) LRA 1925, in which case he is bound because it *is* an overriding interest. Here, as discussed previously, it is unlikely that Janet will be able to establish a para (g) overriding interest, and therefore it seems that if there is an estoppel licence the question whether it is binding on the building company will turn on whether or not it has been entered as a notice or caution on the register. Finally, if Janet has an estoppel licence there is no certainty as to what relief will be granted by the court to satisfy the equity (ie what remedy she will get). In this regard, the courts have shown great flexibility (remedies used include transfer of fee simple to licensee; life interest for licensee; and reimbursement of licensee's expenses). However, this in turn has produced uncertainty because it is difficult for practitioners to anticipate how the equity will be satisfied in a given case.

In conclusion, it seems that Janet's best hope for resisting the building company's effort to gain possession of the house would be to try to establish an estoppel licence. However, it is by no means certain that such a licence can be found here.

References

(1) [1972] 1 WLR 301
(2) [1984] 1 All ER 244
(3) [1990] 2 WLR 867
(4) [1986] 3 WLR 114
(5) [1990] 2 WLR 832
(6) [1936] 3 All ER 483
(7) [1952] 1 All ER 149
(8) [1988] 2 All ER 147

QUESTION 8

General Comment

A rather tricky question which covers modified fee simples and one of the essential requirements for a valid lease. Part (a) is particularly challenging and probably requires more consideration than the other two parts of the question.

Skeleton Solution

a) Legal estates – s1(1) LPA 1925.
   Modified fee simples.
   Effect of determinable fee simple.
   Strict settlements.
   Power of sale of tenant for life.
   Section 106 SLA 1925, *Re Acklom*.

b) Lease for life – s149(6) LPA 1925.

c) Term or duration of a lease must be certain.
   Lace v *Chantler*, *Prudential Assurance Co Ltd* v *London Residuary Body*.
   Tenancy at will.
   Periodic tenancy.

Suggested Solution

The question requires consideration of three separate dispositions, each of which is considered in turn. The first part concerns modified fee simples and aspects of strict settlements while parts two and three deal with one of the essential requirements for a valid lease.

a) Since 1 January 1926, only two estates are capable of existing at law – the freehold and the leasehold (s1(1) Law of Property Act (LPA) 1925). The technical legal name for a freehold is an 'estate in fee simple absolute in possession'. 'Fee' means inheritable, 'simple' inheritable generally and, crucially for the purposes of this part of the question, the word 'absolute' is used in its accustomed sense (ie the estate is unencumbered and will continue for ever). The word 'absolute' distinguishes a fee simple from a modified fee simple such as a determinable fee simple or a conditional fee simple.

Here the disposition is Blackacre to Alice 'in fee simple for as long as she lives on Blackacre'. Thus it is less than absolute and cannot be a legal estate (the phrase 'lives on' is a little curious and has been construed by the author as meaning 'resides at'). It is submitted that the phrase 'as long as' describes a duration of time, rather than a contingency, and therefore the disposition would rank as a determinable fee simple rather than a fee simple subject to a condition subsequent. A determinable fee simple is a fee simple which will automatically determine on the occurrence of some specified event which may not happen. If the specified event does occur the fee determines and the land reverts to the original grantor or his heirs. The grantor of a determinable fee simple retains a possibility of reverter (ie that if the specified event does occur the land reverts to the grantor). Words such as 'while', 'during', and 'so long as' are apt for the creation of a determinable fee.

Since a determinable fee simple is less than absolute it cannot take effect as a legal estate (s1(1) LPA 1925) (a fee made determinable under the School Sites Acts may be legal but this is not relevant here). Accordingly, the grant to Alice takes effect as an equitable estate (s1(3) LPA 1925), with the legal estate remaining in the grantor. Therefore, Blackacre stands limited in trust for Alice for a determinable fee. As such there is a strict settlement (s1 Settled Land Act (SLA) 1925). Alice is the person entitled to exercise the powers of tenant for life under the Settled Land Act (s20 SLA 1925), and as such she is entitled to call for the legal estate. If she does get in the legal estate then the threat of determination might rank as an inhibition dissuading her from exercising her statutory power of sale, and to the extent that it is in fact an inhibition then it is void. This is because s106 SLA 1925 renders void any attempt by a settlor to dissuade or prohibit the tenant for life from using his powers.

Sometimes strict settlements provide that the tenant for life will forfeit his interest if he ceases to reside on the settled land. The view of case law of such a provision is that if the tenant for life ceases to reside on the settled land for some reason other than the exercise of his statutory powers (eg he prefers to live elsewhere), then the provision for forfeiture is operative and he loses his interest. However if the reason for him ceasing to reside is that he has exercised his statutory powers, eg by selling the land, then there is no forfeiture and he continues to be entitled as tenant for life, receiving in the latter situation the income from the purchase money (*Re Acklom* (1) and *Re Aberconway's ST* (2)).

Accordingly, if Alice decides to exercise her tenant-for-life power of sale (so that she will need to give vacant possession and so cease to reside at Blackacre), then the possibility of reverter would de facto inhibit her and would be void. On the possibility of reverter having become void Alice is now entitled to the legal fee simple absolute as tenant for life to add to her equitable fee simple – the determinable fee having ceased to be determinable. Therefore, she is now the sole legal and beneficial owner of Blackacre and the strict settlement comes to an end. If, on the other hand, Alice ceases to reside at Blackacre for reasons unconnected with the exercise of her powers as tenant for life, then the determining event has occurred, her fee terminates and the beneficial ownership of Blackacre reverts to the grantor.

b) One of the requirements for there to be a valid legal lease is that both the commencement date, and the duration of the term, must be certain or capable of being ascertained at the outset of the term (s205(1)(xxvii) LPA 1925). This requirement means that a lease for life would fall foul of this principle and be void. However, in respect of such a type of lease, statute has intervened to prevent this happening. By virtue of s149(6) LPA 1925 a lease at a rent for life or determinable on life is converted into a term of 90 years, determinable by notice served after the dropping of the life. Accordingly, Bert gets a 90-year term but the landlord can give notice to terminate after Bert's death.

c) Here it is again necessary to emphasise that in order for a lease to be a valid legal one it must have a certain duration (ie its ultimate date of expiry must be ascertainable at or before the commencement of the term). In *Lace* v *Chantler* (3) a lease granted during the course of the Second World War for the duration of the war was void. However, several Court of Appeal decisions in recent years cast some doubt on this principle. For example, *Re Midland Railway Company's Agreement* (4) decided that the landlord could bar himself from determining the lease. This case was applied by the Court of Appeal in *Ashburn Anstalt* v *Arnold* (5). The principle of *Lace* v *Chantler* was reaffirmed by the House of Lords in *Prudential Assurance Co Ltd* v *London Residuary Body* (6). There their Lordships held that a lease 'until land was required for widening the road' was void because the period was uncertain.

Lord Templeman said of *Re Midland Railway Company's Agreement* that if it was correctly decided it would make it unnecessary for a lease to be of a certain duration. However, their Lordships held that it had been wrongly decided and it was overruled (*Ashburn Anstalt* v *Arnold* was also overruled on this point).

Accordingly, if the day of the next General Election has been fixed before this lease commences then it is a valid lease. If, however, the day of the next General Election has not been fixed then the purported lease is ineffective for the purpose of creating a term. If this purported lease is ineffective to grant a term then it would take effect as a contractual licence to occupy. If Calum goes into possession, with both parties intending a lease, then possession with intent makes him a tenant at will and if, for example, he pays a weekly rent then it is to be inferred that he becomes a weekly tenant.

References

(1) [1929] 1 Ch 195
(2) [1953] Ch 647
(3) [1944] KB 368
(4) [1971] Ch 725
(5) [1989] Ch 1
(6) [1992] 3 WLR 279